BRAD WIENERS & DAVID PESCOVITZ

REALITY CHECK

W9-BGR-276

You've Heard the Hype.
Wired Asked the Experts.
Here's the Real Future.

Research by Meri Brin
Foreword by Bruce Sterling

1980 1990 **1996** 2000 2010 2020 2030 2040 2050 2060 2070 2080 2090 2100 2110 2120 2130 2140 2150 2160 2170 2180 2190 2200 2210 2220 2225

HARDWIRED SAN FRANCISCO

Other Books from HardWired

Digerati: Encounters with the Cyber Elite, by John Brockman

The Medium is the Massage: An Inventory of Effects, by Marshall McLuhan and Quentin Fiore, produced by Jerome Agel

Mind Grenades: Manifestos from the Future, by John Plunkett and Louis Rossetto

Wired Style: Principles of English Usage in the Digital Age, from the editors of *Wired*, edited by Constance Hale

CONTENTS

There are many easy ways to talk about the future, and this book doesn't use a single one of them.

Prophets and astrologers have known for centuries that if you talk in a sufficiently nebulous fashion, then people will read their own mystic revelations into the verbiage. Stock-market gurus know that you can hedge about either the numbers or the date, but to predict both at once is professionally fatal and will lose you clients in droves. Science fiction writers know that a good gush of ray-gun-blasting melodrama will cover a multitude of futuristic sins.

Reality Check, however, features my very favorite kind of futurism, one that just barges right in and makes all kinds of loud and irrevocable mistakes. There's scarcely any hedging in this book, no motion wasted covering anybody's behind. Wanna know when you'll have holes bored in your head by robot surgeons? 2010! Cheap supersonic flight? 2014! All the drugs you can eat? 2019! Often wrong but never in doubt, this is just the kind of book we need while confronting the rare opportunity of a spanking new millennium.

I consider this book's brand of futurism to be a profoundly healthy approach, one that deserves attention and wide use. At the end of the twentieth century, anybody with two neurons left to rub together has got to know that the future is profoundly unpredictable, even in principle. Mysticism is worse than useless, and the pace of innovation is insane. It's time we junked those conical hats with the stars and crescent moons, and strapped on our motorcycle helmets. The road ahead, glimpsed in fitful moonshine, is a veritable moonscape of potholes. Worse still, the real roadblocks for the status quo are things that can't even show up on today's radar. They're simply unimaginable, like, say, personal computation or AIDS would have been in 1919.

This book is not "the real future," because although it is profoundly weird it is not quite weird enough. A genuine text from, say, the year 2025 would be blisteringly surreal, a slippery plastic tome full of tedious, inexplicable graphs about the impact of remsnorkeling and mudtrufflage on the booming economy of subsaharan Africa. This book, despite its out-there graphic design, is all-too-comprehensible. It's not the future, because it can't be, but it is a whole sizzling stack of today's sexiest ideas about the future, and hunt as you might, you won't find a better treatment of these ideas.

ACKNOWLEDGMENTS THIS BOOK MAY HAVE JUST TWO NAMES ON ITS COVER, BUT IT'S TO THE CREDIT OF MANY THAT
THE PESCOVITZ FAMILY, KELLY SPARKS, JOHN FOX, JANINE SIEJA, ERIC PAULOS, CARLA SINCLAIR, R.U. SIRIUS, LISA PALA
GOLDBERG, TODD LAPPIN, AND TIM BARKOW. BRAD WIENERS IS GRATEFUL TO, AMONG OTHERS, MARY ASHLEY; CHAR-
WIRED RESEARCH DESK; KEVIN "IF YOU'RE GOING TO BE WRONG, BE BOLDLY WRONG" KELLY; CHASE PANTANELLA; JACK
AND BRAD WISH TO FURTHER THANK PETER RUTTEN FOR THE OPPORTUNITY AND HIS GUIDANCE; DONNA LINDEN, ALA
AND CARLA RUFF FOR PRODUCING AND PRESENTING THE BOOK; AND, OF COURSE, ALL THE EXPERTS WHO AGREED TO

FOREWORD

A lot of interesting people think seriously about the future, but they never fail to become deeply embarrassed when asked to crawl down from Olympus and make some honest, rule-of-thumb, cash-on-the-barrelhead predictions. However, if they're put on a panel, where responsibility is safely diffused and the differences are split, quite remarkable insights can emerge. The common wisdom isn't really held by anybody; the common wisdom is an emanation of entirely mythical creatures like the Average Voter. *Reality Check* is a common-wisdom generator.

And yet, the dozens of people polled in this book are not entirely mythical creatures. They are commonly legendary figures in their own fields, people who truly are as good at this sort of thing as anybody anywhere can be expected to get.

People just don't come any smarter than Denise Caruso (journalist, conference maven), John Markoff (journalist, true-crime reporter), and Donald Norman (interface guru). For that matter, there aren't too many flies on Derrick de Kerckhove (media theorist), Danny Hillis (supercomputer designer), or Richard Smalley (chemist), either. There is a host of other equally distinguished scholars, researchers, and industrialists in this book. It's also pleasant to see the presence here of the late Dr. Timothy Leary, perhaps the twentieth century's single greatest visionary charlatan, a guy whose ability to register and manipulate popular trends was almost supernatural. Dr. Tim actually *deserved* a conical hat with stars.

This is a book about the future which, in delicious irony, is entirely and utterly of the present. There are always more big waves in the ocean, but if you're going to surf you have to pick your moment. This book is of this moment. There are websurfing links galore in here, making it not so much a book as a beach. Thanks to the advent of the Internet and World Wide Web, you can pick and surf the most interesting futuristic topics at your own convenience. You can web-surf them right away, during that delicate instant of history before the URLs all shift, the connections fail, the files shift addresses, and the hotlinks give way to the curse of link-rot.

And if you find some of these predictions a little far-out, a bit hard to grasp and credit, just imagine quoting that last sentence to somebody in 1975. See what I mean?

Bruce Sterling

CAME TO BE. DAVID PESCOVITZ THANKS STEVE STEINBERG, MARK FRAUENFELDER, DOUGLAS RUSHKOFF, MAGAZINE, JON HUGHES, DR. MANFRED WOLFRAM, TIMOTHY FERRIS, IARA LEE, GEORGE GUND III, KEN M, CLARK, MEGANN, AND BRIAN; WALTER WIENERS AND PENNY POPE; MERI BRIN; STEVE, TIM, AND THE PIER; MIRIAM WOLF; THE CITY MAG GANG; AND DOMINIQUE "LE FUTUR" PARENT-ALTIER. BOTH DAVID CHE, SUSANNA DULKINYS, AMY HOWORTH, ERIC RODENBECK, JENNIFER COLTON, ALEXANDRA McOSKER, ON THE RECORD.

GENETICALLY ENGINEERED WEAPONS OF WAR

1996

Advances in biotechnology and the imminent completion of the Human Genome Project (see page 147) have not only produced excitement at the prospect of better medicine and longer, healthier lives, but also anxiety over the proliferation of a new breed of biological weapons that will affect present and future generations alike. Fortunately, these anxieties have played out mostly in fiction, like the unstoppable infection of Stephen King's *The Stand*.

According to the experts we consulted, there is cause for concern, if not panic. In fact, two of our experts claim that genetic engineering has already been put to the task of developing new viruses that attack a potential enemy's body "from within," and because they are new, no vaccine or antidote exists.

So far, efforts to curb the production and proliferation of chemical and biological weapons – including those that are genetically engineered – have been ineffective. In 1987, 18 years after President Richard Nixon signed a ban on R & D of chemical and biological weapons, the U.S. Department of Defense admitted to funding 127 sites conducting such weapons research. Meanwhile, U.S. spies suspect as many as 11 countries to be actively developing biological and chemical weapons, and, in at least one case, have been proved correct. In September 1995, Robin Wright of the *Los Angeles Times* disclosed that Iraq, in blatant defiance of the United Nations, had devoted extensive resources (including 150 scientists) to the development of several viruses, including ones engineered to cause ocular bleeding and chronic diarrhea.

Today, the U.S. government claims that the US$1.4 billion managed by the U.S. Army through the Pentagon's Joint Program for Biological Defense is devoted not to R & D, but to detection and investigation technologies and mass production of vaccines against biological warfare agents. And it is participating in talks co-chaired by Hungary's Ambassador Tibor Toth and Australia's Ambassador for Disarmament, Richard Starr, on how to make the 1975 Biological Weapons Convention (BWC) more binding. The BWC lacks both provisions for verification of compliance and the ability to punish violators.

U.S. Targets New Biological Weapons Threats: Department of Defense news on what is being as many as weapons news area page. www.cbdcom.apgea.army.mil/ Chemical Warfare/Chemical and Biological Defense Command: Homepage of a special military division. www.doc.dtic.dla.mil/dtic U.S. Army Chemical and Biological Defense Command: Homepage of a special military division. www.stcnet.com Biological Defense Information Analysis Center (CBIAC): Jeanne M. Rosser introduces this agency and discusses its work to date. www.stcnet.com /digest/digest95-3/cbiac.html STC Biological Research Activities: Field tests of vaccines and other preventive measures against biological weapons. www.novo.dk/enzymes/advent.html /projects/biores.html The Advent of Genetic Engineering: A serviceable introduction to genetic engineering. www.novo.dk/enzymes/advent.html

RICHARD GARWIN, CHAIR OF THE FAS FUND, THE RESEARCH ARM OF THE FEDERATION OF AMERICAN SCIENTISTS, CONSULTANT TO THE U.S. DEPARTMENT OF DEFENSE

JOHN ALEXANDER, PH.D., RETIRED U.S. ARMY COLONEL, AND HEAD OF THE NONLETHAL WEAPONRY PROGRAM AT LOS ALAMOS NATIONAL LABORATORY

MANUEL DE LANDA, AUTHOR OF *WAR IN THE AGE OF INTELLIGENT MACHINES*

1988 1989 1990 1991 1992 1993 1994 1995 **1996** 1997 1998 1999 2000 2001 2002 2003 2004 2005 2006 2007 2008 2009 2010 2011 2012 2013 2014

AFFORDABLE HOME CD RECORDERS

1997

Ironstone Technologies: A purveyor of CD-ROM and optical storage devices. www.ironstone.mb.ca/infopage/item.html CD-Recorders: Kinfronics CD-Recorders and Software: A manufacturer's info with an emphasis on the batch aspect of CD recording. www.kintronics.com/CDR.html Dolby Laboratories: Informative, "we love what we do" home page to one of the world's leading sound engineering firms. www.dolby.com/ Toshiba – DVD Format Unification: Announcing the DVD, the format that may have a profound effect on CD use in the future. www.toshiba.co.jp/about/press/ 1995_12/pro8o2.html DAT – General Questions and Formats: The basics on DAT, digital audio tape, in a Q & A format. www.execpc.com/%7Eporettma/faqt.html

PETER GOTCHER, PRESIDENT AND CEO, DIGIDESIGN, INC.

IVAN BERGER, TECHNICAL EDITOR, AUDIO MAGAZINE

RON GOMPERTZ, PRESIDENT, HEYDAY RECORDS, CO-CREATOR OF CYBORGASM

JERRY HARRISON, AUDIO PRODUCER AND FORMER TALKING HEAD

ROGER DRESSLER, TECHNICAL DIRECTOR, DOLBY LABORATORIES

Imagine owning a CD player that not only plays music but, like a cassette tape deck, enables you to record it as well. With it you could record music from a variety of sources while taking advantage of the CD's superior sound quality and durability. Now imagine that this home CD recorder costs about the same as a VCR.

The only obstacle to this scenario stems from concerns about copyright infringement. Of course, there is a well-known precedent for copyright hysteria slowing an audio technology's mass acceptance: digital audio tape, or DAT. The experience with DAT leads Roger Dressler to believe that CD recorders will be kept pricey in an effort to prevent artists' work from getting bootlegged.

Unlike DAT, however, CDs are already in regular use, both by audiophiles and computer users, and our other panelists believe that the desire to record on them will overwhelm the protectionists. Because of two irresistible forces in the market – computer users who are eager to record their own CD-ROMs and innovations like DVD (the CD's answer to the double-density floppy disk) – our experts say that it's just a matter of months before CD recorders, already available to those willing to spend US$2,500, become available to those with a more modest budget of US$250–500.

MOVIES-ON-DEMAND

1997

URLS/FURTHER READING

Intel Scalable Systems Division: A slightly dated paper on what Intel intends to do via the convergence of cable, telephone, and television. *www.ssd.intel.com/IMS /techb.html* Audio and Video on Demand: The ATM switch and other tips. *wwwmcb.cs.colorado.edu/home/homenii/demand.html* Interactive Video Services: A highly informative if not entirely inspired discussion of video-on-demand technology by Eric Arnum, editor of *Telecommunications Report*. *www.sequent.com/public/mktg /whpapers/vidond/vidond.html#on* Video-on-Demand: An overview of the developmental and marketing issues. *www.cs.tut.fi/tlt/stuff/vod/VoDOverview/vod.html*

DERRICK DE KERCKHOVE, DIRECTOR OF THE MCLUHAN PROGRAM, THE UNIVERSITY OF TORONTO

MAURICE WELSH, DIRECTOR OF NEW MEDIA MARKET DEVELOPMENT, PACIFIC BELL

MICHAEL SCHARGE, MIT MEDIA LAB FELLOW, CONTRIBUTING EDITOR FOR *I.D. MAGAZINE*

JOHN BRINGENBERG, DIRECTOR OF BUSINESS DEVELOPMENT, TELE-COMMUNICATIONS, INC.

BENJAMIN BRITTON, ASSISTANT PROFESSOR OF FINE ARTS AND ELECTRONIC ARTS AT THE UNIVERSITY OF CINCINNATI'S COLLEGE OF DESIGN, ART, ARCHITECTURE AND PLANNING

Blame the incredible success of Blockbuster Video, but ever since it became possible to transmit digital images via modem, the buzz about the prospect of ordering and downloading a movie over the Net – "movies-on-demand" – has been one of the prospective "killer apps" that wouldn't quit.

As with anything, the real-world prospects for this convenience largely depend on the expectations set for it. If, for example, one is content to select from an online inventory and physically pick up a videocassette later, movies-on-demand is already here. If, however, one insists on desktop downloading capability, then several hurdles must yet be overcome.

First, consumers will have to possess or have access to the bandwidth necessary to receive digitized video efficiently (see "Fiber to the Home," page 65). Second, movie buffs will need technology – whether it be a powerful PC with a high-resolution monitor or "smart" TV – that displays digitized video as well as or better than TVs do video on cassettes today. Third, providers of movies-on-demand services will not only have to be cost-competitive with cable TV and rental outlets like Blockbuster, but also make movie audiences aware that they are. Fourth, providers will have to reckon with the fact that the digital format will allow computer users to copy and manipulate movies in ways that VCR owners can't even imagine today. Finally, as our experts point out, the providers of movies-on-demand services face a technical challenge: how to accelerate data rates – the speeds at which the recorded video and audio travel over the Net. To do this will require increases in the speed of network access (from their server to the user's server) and improvements in image compression, so that the files take less time to transmit and require less bandwidth.

For his part, Derrick de Kerckhove considers movies-on-demand "one of the least interesting services" the Net can provide, adding that it is an attempt to have the Net replace a service – whether via satellite, cable, or video rental shop – that is already fairly mature. Instead, de Kerckhove would rather see energy devoted to developing a service upon which the Net would clearly improve. De Kerckhove and Benjamin Britton also suggest that satellite services might preclude online movies-on-demand.

1993 1994 1995 1996 1996 1996 **1997** 1998 1999 2000 2001 2002 2003 2004 2005 2006 2007 2008 2009 2010 2011 2012 2013 2014 2015 2016 2017

INTELLIGENT AGENTS

1997

Depending on how you define "intelligent agents," they either remain a fantasy or a prototype, or they have been with us for some time. The humblest intelligent agents, for example, could include spellcheckers and virus detectors. "Smarter" examples already in wide use include bozo filters (programs that function like a secretary, selecting whose email gets through to your mailbox); programs that comb the Internet while you are away or otherwise engaged, thereby simplifying and reducing your research efforts; and agents that alert you to activity in a news group that you subscribe to.

Of course, if you define intelligent agents as software that "thinks for itself," their reality remains more embryonic – like "bots." As Andrew Leonard writes in *Bots: The Origin of New Species*, "strictly speaking, all bots are 'autonomous' – able to react to their environments and make decisions without prompting their creators.... Most bot connoisseurs consider true bots to be more than mindless ones and zeros. Even more important than function is behavior – bona fide bots are programs with personality. Real bots talk, make jokes, have feelings – even if those feelings are nothing more than cleverly conceived algorithms."

In choosing a year when intelligent agents would reach a mass market, the semantics of the term proved the determining factor for our experts. Notes Don Norman: "It depends on the meaning of intelligent, which is always elusive. We have agents now. Ten years ago they were called intelligent. Not today." Denise Caruso considers intelligent agents to be those that are more closely linked to the user, such as computers equipped with voice and handwriting recognition (see page 29). If it's an information-retrieval service people want, she notes, "they're already here."

Internet Sortbot: site on research being done on bots, introduced for the newbie. *www.cs.washington.edu/research/projects/sotbots/www.sotbots.htm*

The Experimental Knowledge Systems Laboratory: Info on an elaborate research facility at the University of Massachusetts. *eksl-www.cs.umass.edu/eksl.html*

World Wide Web Robots, Wanderers, and Spiders: An easy-to-follow introduction with a bibliography. *info.webcrawler.com/mak/projects/robots /robots.html* **Intelligent Robotics Laboratory:** All kinds of robots under construction at Vanderbilt University. *shogun.vuse.vanderbilt.edu/CIS/IRL/*

Intelligent Software Agents: A thorough treatment organized along an academic outline. *www.itsnet.com/~sterling/agent/agenttoc.html*

ROBERT JACOBSON, FOUNDER AND PRESIDENT, WORLDESIGN, INC.

DON NORMAN, VICE PRESIDENT, ADVANCED TECHNOLOGY, APPLE COMPUTER

DENISE CARUSO, DIGITAL COMMERCE COLUMNIST FOR *THE NEW YORK TIMES*, EXECUTIVE PRODUCER OF THE SPOTLIGHT CONFERENCE ON INTERACTIVE MEDIA

JOHN MARKOFF, REPORTER, *THE NEW YORK TIMES*, AUTHOR OF *CYBERPUNKS: OUTLAWS AND HACKERS ON THE COMPUTER FRONTIER*

1992 1993 1994 1995 1996 **1997** 1997 1998 1999 2000 2001 2002 2003 2004 2005 2006 2007 2008 2009 2010 2011 2012 2013 2014 2015 2016 2017

/home.html **Mark Twain Bank: A bank offering e-cash services and information for the uninitiated.** *www.marktwain.com/* **Conditional Access for Europe (CAFE):** **Making Europe safe for e-cash.** *www.cwi.nl/cwi/projects/cafe.html* **Sandia National Labs, Electronic Cash: An electronic cash system that incorporates trustee-based tracing so no one but you can spend your digital cash.** *www.cs.sandia.gov/HPCCIT/el_cash.html* **Mondex: Homepage of provider of electronic cash cards.** *www .mondex.com/mondex/home.html*

"What is digital money?" ask Daniel C. Lynch and Leslie Lundquist in their book *Digital Money: The New Era of Internet Commerce*. Their reply: "Digital money is an electronic replacement for cash. It is storable, transferable, and unforgeable. It is the cuneiform of a new age. As it is written on the DigiCash homepage, digital money is 'numbers that are money'."

With e-cash, it's been said, you will be able to do everything you do with hard currency, except flip a coin. And it will enable you to do what you can't do with spare change: buy stuff over the Net.

The idea is simply to have your bank issue the money you need for transactions in digital form – whether encoded on a debit card, or made available over the Net, as several services already do.

With help from Lynch and Lundquist, here's how a digital cash transaction goes: as a client of the bank, you submit your request to the bank via a large, encrypted number that represents a discreet value (US$20, say), with your digital signature attached. Your bank would debit your account in the amount of 20 digital clams, and then would sign and return the encrypted number (*sans* your digital signature), which you then forward to the payee. The payee's bank can then use the number to reverify the transaction and deposit US$20 into the payee's account. A lot of steps, perhaps, but all but a few are completely automated and secure.

The pivotal enabling technology for e-cash, of course, is cryptography: the ability to make the money safe in transit – technology that is already here. Technical hurdles, however, are not why our experts predict it will take a couple of years before e-cash really catches on. (In fact, David Chaum, founder of DigiCash and J. S. Boggs, a fine artist whose work focuses on currency, both note that paper money is not safe from tampering and that digital money will be harder to hack than paper). E-cash mavens anticipate resistance from the public, and from banks as well, who may be loath to see a reduction in their credit card business. Says Fred Schneider of Andersen Consulting: "Anonymity in conducting transactions will be a big benefit of electronic cash, but loss of credit float for current credit users will be a barrier."

Back | Forward | Home | Reload | Images | Open | Print | Find | Stop

merilyn moore

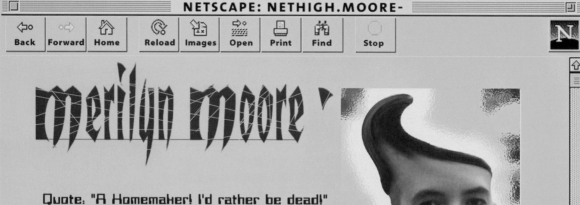

Quote: "A Homemaker! I'd rather be dead!"
—Lisa Simpson
Academic: Class Valedictorian
Activities: Editor, Cyber HS Yearbook on
CD; Member, Paper Preservation Society
Chicago, IL
meri@moore.com

jimmy montage

Quote: "The best way to predict the futute
is to create it."—Alan Hay
Academic: 3.1 GPA
Activities: Member, HHOS, Hacker's
Forum; Member, Motorcross, Voted Class
Clown :-P
Phoenix, AZ
jimmy@curtis.net

FIRST VIRTUAL HIGH SCHOOL GRADUATING CLASS

1998

The Globewide Network Academy: A course catalog for a "global classroom." *uu-gna.mit.edu:8001/uu-gna/index.html* Virtual Online University: A major resource for online education with K-12 curricula and an introduction to Athena University. *www.athena.edu/index.html* Global SchoolNet Foundation: Excellent resources for kids displayed on a well-organized site, including info on International Schools CyberFair. *www.gsn.org/* Edison Project: A partnership looking to test ways of using the Net in vocational, academic, and bilingual education. *whyy.org/~edison/* The Net School Group: Coalition of schools that offer education over the Net. *netschool.edu/*

At first glance, there isn't a teenager alive who wouldn't like to go to high school without actually having to *go* to school. Instead of alarm clocks, cramped school buses, locker room embarrassments, and 45- to 50-minute periods of mandatory boredom, students could enroll in courses, submit homework, and earn a degree over the Net. (One can already imagine the high-tech excuses: "Sorry, teach, a bot ate my homework.")

And the appeal of virtual high school is not only to teenagers. Plenty of pundits now decry the state of public schools and suggest that parents take an alternative approach to educating their children: "home schooling," a process that a PC connected to the Net would surely enhance.

Whatever the reason – residence in a foreign country or in a remote location, or disdain for the quality of education offered at the local high school – attendance is up online. At present, several universities offer courses on the World Wide Web, and a few include resources for students in grades K–12.

Though they applaud these services, especially for those without a school or easy library access, the experts we consulted didn't think that a completely virtual high school was such a bright idea. Even if virtual school is viable (as are the radio and mail correspondence courses that have survived for years), Allison Alltucker objects that the personal teacher-student relationship will suffer if long-distance education increases. Nevertheless, Alltucker concedes that it would be easier to customize curricula to meet individual students' needs on a computer than it is in a classroom of 25 kids. Then again, Marcia Linn suggests that a virtual high school might not be favored by kids, after all. "A virtual high school," says Linn, "will be about as appealing to teens as the virtual mall."

1991
1992
1993
1994
1995
1996 MARCIA C. LINN, DIRECTOR OF THE INSTITUTIONAL TECHNOLOGY PROGRAM AND PROFESSOR OF MATHEMATICS, UC BERKELEY
1996 LEWIS PERELMAN, EXECUTIVE EDITOR, KNOWLEDGE, INC. AND AUTHOR OF *SCHOOL'S OUT* (AVON BOOKS)
1997
1998
1999 WILL JONES, PRESIDENT OF THE NATIONAL INSTITUTE FOR TECHNOLOGY IN EDUCATION
1999 GARY KIDD, SUPERINTENDENT OF SCHOOLS, CENTER CONSOLIDATED SCHOOL DISTRICT, COLORADO
2000
2001
2002 ALLISON ALLTUCKER, EDUCATIONAL TECHNOLOGY SPECIALIST, THE EDISON PROJECT
2003
2004
2005
2006
2007
2008
2009
2010
2011
2012
2013
2014
2015

FLAT-RATE PHONE SERVICE
1998

Long a dream of anyone involved in a long-distance romance, flat-rate phone charges have been a staple of local telephone service for decades, and the source of unwarranted hype for nearly as long. Will flat-rate service ever become as standard for long distance as it is for local toll calls? The experts we consulted are divided, but three of five say yes.

Unless phone systems are nationalized, Benjamin Britton believes, phone rates will never be "flatter" than they are right now. Nonetheless, thinking out loud, Britton does foresee the possibility that in the future telephone service subscribers might pay a greater part of their monthly bill for increased bandwidth (see also "Fiber to the Home," page 65), as opposed to long distance. And, as phone companies see greater bandwidth as a major source of new revenue, they might reduce or "flatten" long-distance rates as an incentive to keep online consumers on the line.

Citing competition among Baby Bells and phone companies' desire to provide Internet connection service, John Bringenberg and Michael Scharge see flat-rate phone service as imminent.

URLS/FURTHER READING
Telecom Industry History: An informative timeline on the history of the field compiled by Blumenfeld & Cohen. *www.clark.net/pub/techlaw/telephony.html* **Alexander Graham Bell's Path to the Telephone.** *jefferson.village.virginiaedu/albell/introduction.html* **Sprint Sense: A promotion from the long-distance carrier Sprint to simplify a user's long distance bills.** *www.sprint.com/home/product/home_dom/sense.html* **AT&T – Military Connect 'N Save: A promotion from AT&T for military personnel and their families so they can reach out and touch each other.** *www.att.com/press/0496/960402.csa.html*

1988

1989

1990

1991

1992

1993

1994

1995

1996 JOHN BRINGENBERG, DIRECTOR OF BUSINESS DEVELOPMENT AT TELE-COMMUNICATIONS, INC.

1997

1998 MICHAEL SCHARGE, MIT MEDIA LAB FELLOW AND CONTRIBUTING EDITOR FOR *I.D. MAGAZINE*

1999 MAURICE WELSH, DIRECTOR OF NEW MEDIA MARKET DEVELOPMENT AT PACIFIC BELL

2000

2001

2002

2003

2004

2005

2006

2007

2008

2009

2010

2011

2012

UNLIKELY DERRICK DE KERCKHOVE, DIRECTOR OF THE MCLUHAN PROGRAM AT THE UNIVERSITY OF TORONTO

NEVER BENJAMIN BRITTON, ASSISTANT PROFESSOR OF FINE ARTS AND ELECTRONIC ARTS AT THE UNIVERSITY OF CINCINNATI'S COLLEGE OF DESIGN, ART, ARCHITECTURE AND PLANNING

MALE BIRTH CONTROL PILL

1999

Fair is fair: if a woman can swallow a pill and alter her body's chemistry such that she can't get pregnant, why shouldn't there be a chemical or hormone men can take to neutralize their seed?

Even though it has been cited (perhaps not incorrectly) as a sexist excuse, it *is* true that engineering a method to deactivate sperm is biologically more difficult than disrupting a woman's monthly egg output. And it isn't as though attempts at a pill for men haven't been made; several male birth control regimens have entered trials, only to prove toxic or to have intolerable side effects such as impotence. Isadora Alman says that some of the trials have confirmed persistent suspicions that men are content to leave birth control to their partners. For instance, the only side effect of one pill that did well in trials, Alman says, is that it turned the eyes of its taker pink. For Alman, this hardly rates when compared to the bloating, risk of cancer, and other myriad side effects associated with the female birth control pill. In fact, she says, this neo-pink eye would actually be an advantage: a woman could tell on sight if her partner or liaison was actually on the pill.

As of this writing, a couple of promising new developments have been made public: Research Triangle Institute in North Carolina has announced a new male contraceptive compound, now in trials, and an Australian group at the Royal Women's Hospital and Melbourne's Prince Henry's Institute of Medical Research has announced male contraceptive injections. The injections, reminiscent of those developed for women, have proven as effective in weekly doses as a woman's daily pill. To make the injections more market-friendly, researchers are trying to make them monthly or quarterly.

In general, our experts are optimistic. They acknowledge gender bias in contraceptive R & D. For example, they pointed to a double standard: to merit financial support, new contraceptive techniques for men must also protect against HIV infection, whereas new contraceptive techniques for women that don't block HIV, such as Norplant, routinely receive funding. But, they insist, men *do* care about birth control – vasectomies, for example, have never been performed more frequently – and they have confidence that a chemical or hormone supplement will soon make it that much easier for men to wear the pants in family planning.

Research Triangle Institute: Male Contraceptive Compound developed: Press reports from the makers of a new compound that has so far proven nontoxic ... nontoxic and effective in rendering rats and mice sterile. www.rti.org/hypo_etc/bc_male.html Contraceptive Options for Men: An engaging, helpful list for those who hate condoms and aren't ready for a vasectomy. www.pregnant.com/kgc/bc/contr_m.htm Men's Contraception Injections Match Pill's Effectiveness: Report on a therapy successful in trials in New South Wales, Australia. www.ozemail.com.au/search/26852.html Ask Isadora: Homepage of the columnist and sexpert with a daily question culled from her columns. www.askisadora.com/

NANCIE S. MARTIN, PRESIDENT OF JOUISANCE PRODUCTIONS AND FORMER EDITOR OF *PLAYGIRL*

ISADORA ALMAN, "ASK ISADORA" SYNDICATED COLUMNIST AND SEX AND RELATIONSHIP COUNSELOR

HOWARD RHEINGOLD, AUTHOR OF *VIRTUAL COMMUNITY, VIRTUAL REALITY* AND EDITOR OF *THE MILLENNIUM WHOLE EARTH CATALOG*

RICHARD KADREY, EDITOR OF *COVERT CULTURE SOURCEBOOK,* AND AUTHOR OF *KAMIKAZE L'AMOUR*

1995 1996 1997 1998 **1999** 1999 2000 2001 2002 2003 2004 2005 2006 2007 2008 2009 2010 2011 2012 2013 2014 2015 2016 2017 2018 2019 2020

BOTTOM LINE: DOZENS OF UNDERPUBLICIZED MALE CONTRACEPTIVE TECHNIQUES CURRENTLY EXIST, BUT IF IT'S THE SIMPLICITY OF A PILL OR INJECTION YOU WANT, LOOK TO 1999.

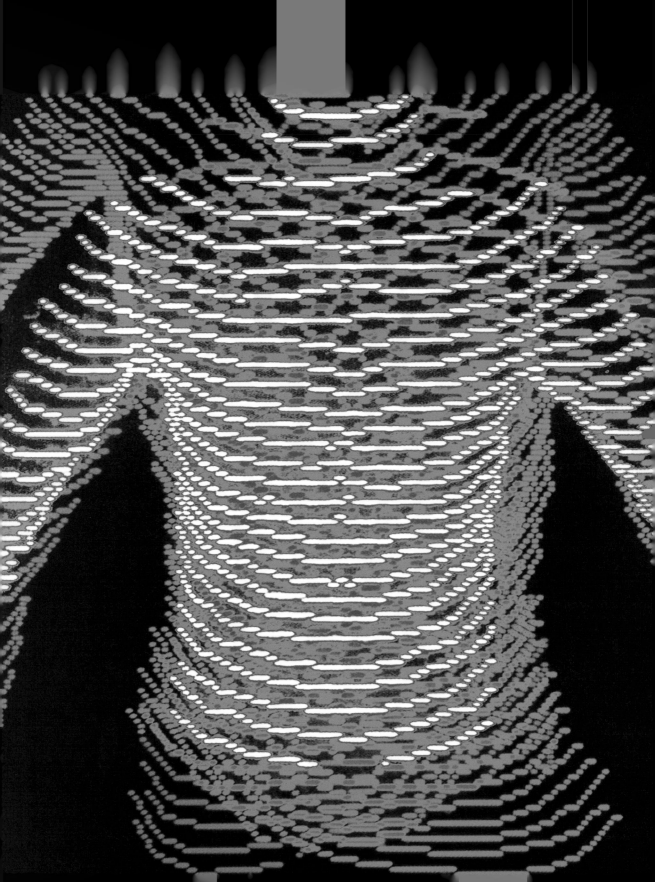

OVERNIGHT CUSTOM CLOTHING

1999

URLS/FURTHER READING
CAD Cut: Technology for hire that computerizes manual processes and produces goods more efficiently. *plainfield.bypass.com/bypass/users/cadcut/cadcut2.html* **[TC]₂ Body Measurement System: Homepage of the system under development by Reality Checker Jud Early.** *dama.tcz.com/ bms.htm* **Interactive Fit Guide: Service from Levis that allows patient buyers to custom fit their jeans.** *www.tui.co.uk/Tuilevis.html* **The Industrial and Social Impact of New Technology in the Clothing Industry into the 2000s: A dissertation on technology and haberdashery.** *www.dratex.co.uk/publications/clotech.html*

Research by the Textile/Clothing Technology Corporation confirms what many of us have known for some time: half of all Americans buy clothing off the rack that doesn't fit.

In an effort to make custom clothing as easy and convenient as bargain hunting, engineers are developing digital body scanners that are more accurate than tape measures and would enable haberdashers to deliver custom clothing overnight and/or expedite custom apparel orders from remote manufacturers.

According to our experts, this technology is well on its way. Haysun Hahn reports that Adidas has begun testing a digital foot scanner for measuring shoe sizes, and that men's stores already tailor dress shirts from prefab garment sections. Jud Early and his full body scanner have been the focus of national media profiles. Sung Park's company, Custom Clothing Technology Corporation, already delivers Levi's Personal Pair women's jeans in less than three weeks. All that remains, Hahn says, is to organize the process on a larger scale; then "companies will be ready to sell the clothes on QVC" (the home shopping television channel).

As with QVC, the problem with this arrangement is that it disappoints consumers who like to try things on. According to Martha Harkey and Gary Henderson, a combined body scanner and video display will give consumers much the same effect as looking in a mirror. Ingrid Johnson, however, dissents, claiming that "mass-produced clothing will always be cheaper than clothing produced on an individual basis."

1991
1992
1993
1994
1995
1996
1997 SUNG PARK, PRESIDENT, CUSTOM CLOTHING TECHNOLOGY CORP.
1997 HAYSUN HAHN, DIRECTOR, BUREAU DE STYLE, A TREND FORECASTING COMPANY
1998
1999
2000 MARTHA HARKEY AND GARY HENDERSON, FOUNDERS, YANG SNOWBOARD CLOTHING, INC.
2000 JUD EARLY, DIRECTOR OF RESEARCH AND DEVELOPMENT, TEXTILE/CLOTHING TECHNOLOGY CORP.
2001
2002
2003
2004
2005
2006
2007
2008
2009
2010
2011
2012
2013
2014
2015
UNLIKELY INGRID JOHNSON, PROFESSOR AND CHAIR OF THE TEXTILE DEVELOPMENT AND MARKETING DEPARTMENT, FASHION INSTITUTE OF TECHNOLOGY

BOTTOM LINE: CUSTOM ATTIRE, FACILITATED BY DIGITAL SCANNERS AND DRIVEN BY THE EVER-PRESENT DEMAND FOR COMFORTABLE CLOTHES, WILL GO

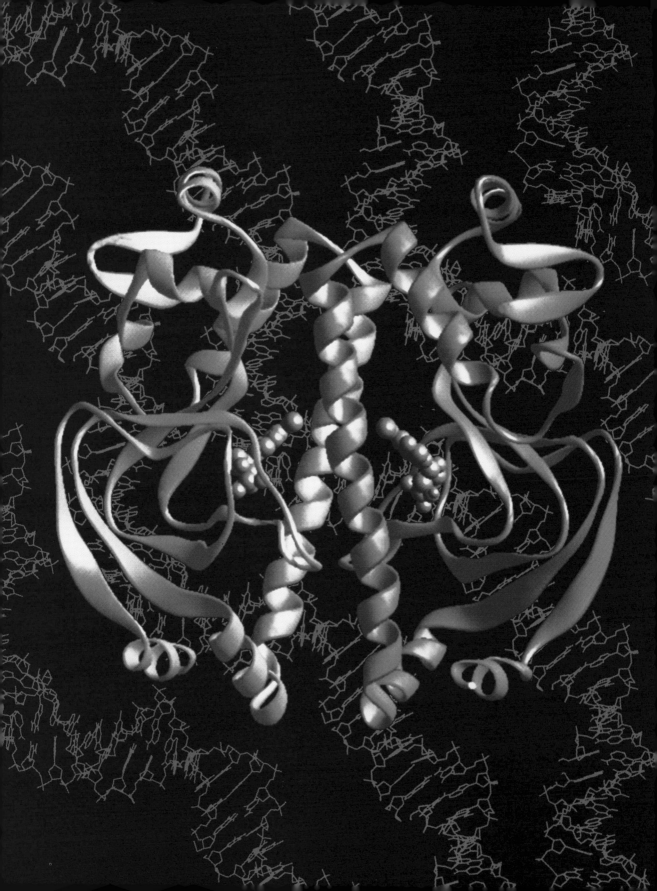

GENE THERAPY FOR CANCER

2000

Cancer remains one of Death's favorite guises. According to the National Cancer Institute, cancer claimed more than 500,000 lives last year – in the United States alone.

Given cancer's many manifestations, numerous studies suggesting that susceptibility to cancer can be inherited, and the many cases in which gene therapy has proven effective, scientists and physicians have turned to genetic research as a potential boon to cancer treatment. Researchers in labs like those at the University of Pittsburgh Cancer Institute (UPCI), where three trials have been conducted in as many years, have seen some promising results.

Led by Dr. Michael Lotze, co-director of the Biological Therapeutics Program, UPCI researchers first proved they could transfer and track a "reporter" gene through a patient's body; they then moved on to a safety trial of interleukin-4, an agent thought to enhance the body's own immune response to cancer. (The trial sought only to identify interleukin-4 dosages that lacked adverse side effects, not to conclude how effective it is at fighting cancer.)

"At the clinical level," they reported, "patients had a variety of responses, including visible reduction in tumor mass and, in a few cases, disappearance of cancer altogether." In 1995, Lotze, along with Dr. Hideaki Tahara, began a gene therapy study with interleukin-12, another agent that enhanced the body's own response to cancer, in patients with advanced cancer.

Among the experts we polled, Dr. David E. R. Sutherland predicts that cancer might be stopped by combining gene therapies with other approaches, such as immunotherapy. Dr. Frank Lee, on the other hand, foresees "sophisticated approaches to deliver functional copies of tumor suppressor genes" – an approach known as immunogenicity.

Even if these experimental therapies prove useful, however, the need for trials will prevent their public availability for at least four more years.

Gene Therapy - Recent Advances: A thorough listing of all of the applications of gene therapy presently in development. www.ncbcp.....ed hgt.org/g......htm
University of Pittsburgh Medical Center: Updates on therapies from a leading research institute. www.upmc.edu/news/genebg.htm Cancer Research Institute:
Homepage to a scientific brain trust. www.cancerresearch.org/ CNS Tumor Research – Immunotherapy: Online kiosk of health information and resources emphasizing
immunotherapy. www.healthtouch.com/level1/leaflets/4425/mindsi16.htm Tumor Suppressor Genes or Antioncogenes: Introduction and fairly technical analysis of
genes that interfere with the development of cancerous tumors. fiona.umsmed.edu/~yar/tumor.html

1992
1993
1994
1995
1996
1997
1998
1999   FRANK LEE, PH.D., MOLECULAR BIOLOGIST
2000   CYNTHIA ROBBINS-ROTH, PH.D., EDITOR-IN-CHIEF OF BIOVENTURE PUBLISHING, INC.
2001
2002
2003
2004
2005
2006
2007
2008
2009
2010
2011
2012
2013
2014
2015
2016
2017

UNKNOWN   DR. DAVID E. R. SUTHERLAND, M.D., PH.D., PROFESSOR OF SURGERY AND DIRECTOR OF THE PANCREAS TRANSPLANT PROGRAM, UNIVERSITY OF MINNESOTA

SOLAR-POWERED AUTOMOBILES

2001

They remain an almost annual feature of television news magazines and sports broadcasts: the wacky, other-worldly sailboat/Formula One vehicles that compete in the Tour de Sol solar car race.

Despite the media attention and the millions in R & D poured into these vehicles, our experts agree that mass-market solar-propelled automobiles won't be parked in our driveways anytime soon – at least, not if you define a solar car as the Tour de Sol does: as a car that owes all of its mobility to the sun. Instead, what they do anticipate – as soon as 2001 – are cars that take advantage of onboard solar-power generators for supplemental power, and the emergence of electric cars that use solar power to recharge their batteries. Solar-powered cars, says Christopher Flavin, *are* electric cars (see "More Than 50% Drive Electric Cars," page 121) in which the sun is a source of electricity.

Donald Osborn, meanwhile, says solar assistance in automotive power will catch on because it will prove vital to long battery life in an age when car batteries are taxed by onboard computers and security systems. He also agrees with Frank Goodman that another beneficial use of solar technology is providing auxiliary power for ventilation while the car is parked.

Steven Strong and Flavin both anticipate that photovoltaic sunroof and rear-spoiler collectors will be incorporated in auto designs within a year or two, and they suggest that those interested in automotive applications of solar power should follow these developments closely.

MIT SEV: National Solar Racing Champions: Homepage of a student organization devoted to building and racing solar and electric cars. www.mit.edu/activities/solar-cars/home.html Solar Car Corporation: Seven years old and counting, this is a tinkerers' corporation out to prove solar and electric retrofits feasible and desirable. www.gaia.org/farm/businesses/scc.html Solar Wave: An R & D program at California State University, Long Beach. www.csulb.edu/~lwarrick/solarwave.html George Washington University Solar Car: Another academically sponsored program. www.seas.gwu.edu/seas/projects/solarcar/index.html Solar-Electric Minicar: Solar Baby invades the British Isles. popularmechanics.com/popmech/tech/U0369B.html

STEVEN STRONG, PRESIDENT, SOLAR DESIGN ASSOCIATES, INC.

THOMAS SUREK, PHOTOVOLTAICS DIVISION, NATIONAL RENEWABLE ENERGY LABORATORY (NREL)

MARK FITZGERALD, COMMUNICATIONS COORDINATOR, NREL

DONALD OSBORN, SUPERVISOR, SACRAMENTO MUNICIPAL UTILITY DISTRICT'S SOLAR PROGRAM

CHRISTOPHER FLAVIN, VICE PRESIDENT FOR RESEARCH, WORLDWATCH INSTITUTE, AND CO-AUTHOR OF *POWER SURGE*

FRANK GOODMAN, MANAGER, PHOTOVOLTAIC TECHNOLOGY AND APPLICATIONS, ELECTRIC POWER RESEARCH INSTITUTE

1994 1995 1996 1997 1998 1998 1998 1999 2000 **2001** 2002 2003 2004 2005 2006 2007 2008 2009 2010 2011 2012 2013 2014 2015 2016 2017 2018

FORTUNE 500 VIRTUAL CORPORATION
2001

"Virtual corporation," a buzzword for years, has come to define some circumstances that Bill Davidow, who is credited with coining the term, probably didn't intend it to. For example, it has been deployed by savvy public relations professionals to sweeten the sound of hostile business takeovers, or to describe third-party businesses that develop software compatible with a larger vendor's programs. By broad definition, a virtual corporation is any business that extends its reach through strategic partnerships, product licensing, and/or branch offices, all of which have been made more feasible by advances in communications.

To get beneath the euphemism and hype, we pinned our experts down concerning the next evolutionary step of a virtual corporation: one without a headquarters. We asked them when they thought companies large enough to be listed on the Fortune 500 list would take full advantage of telecommuting (see page 37) and videoconferencing (see page 35) to eliminate the need for a majority of its staff to assemble in one place each workday.

First, they referred us to a few surveys. According to a 1995 report by Market Research Institute (MRI), for example, almost two-thirds of Fortune 1000 companies have telecommuting programs, but half of them are relatively new, launched after 1993. Of the executives polled at companies with such programs, 92 percent believed that telecommuting benefited employers through cost reduction, increased productivity, and improved employee morale.

Franklin D. Becker predicts that large virtual corporations will maintain multiuse hubs containing meeting space used for teaching new skills to a geographically dispersed workforce, and he agrees with others that newer companies will probably achieve virtual status sooner than companies with a long-standing hometown presence. Tom Newhouse believes that "widely varied human personalities and job skill types" will keep at least half of a company's employees in a main office. "The headquarters," he says, "will be wherever the CEO is."

Andersen Consulting: Homepage to the global consulting firm. www.ac.com/ About Virtual Companies: Resources for going virtual from the Crossroads Project. www.idiscover.co.uk/rodz/virt_co.htm The Virtual Corporation: Can We Ensure the Momentum? The president of a consultant group discusses prospects for and social benefits of virtual corporations. xoweb.xopen.org/opencomments/winter96/1_text.htm Center for Workforce Effectiveness: Homepage of a management consulting firm with articles and briefs intended mostly for prospective clients. www.cwelink.com/index.html

VAN ROMINE, DIRECTOR, INSTITUTE FOR TELEWORK

JOE CARTER, MANAGING DIRECTOR, ANDERSEN CONSULTING CENTER FOR STRATEGIC TECHNOLOGY

N. FREDRIC CRANDALL, PH.D., FOUNDING PARTNER, THE CENTER FOR WORKFORCE EFFECTIVENESS, INC.

TOM NEWHOUSE, OWNER/PRINCIPAL, THOMAS J. NEWHOUSE DESIGN, AN INDUSTRIAL DESIGN FIRM

FRANKLIN D. BECKER, DIRECTOR, INTERNATIONAL WORKPLACE STUDIES PROGRAM, CORNELL UNIVERSITY, AND PARTNER, @WORK CONSULTING GROUP

1992 1993 1994 1995 1996 1997 1998 1999 2000 **2001** 2002 2003 2004 2005 2006 2007 2008 2009 2010 2011 2012 2013 2014 2015 2016 UNLIKELY NEVER

GLOBAL WIRELESS TELEPHONE NUMBER

2001

For multinational businesspeople who need to take their calls literally wherever they go – whether on a Venetian taxi, in the New York subway, or while backpacking in the Himalayas – a hand-held phone connected to a global wireless communications network would be a dream come true. And even though Himalayan mountaineers would really only require a wireless phone to call in a rescue team, the experts we consulted believe this dream of global wireless access will soon come true.

For starters, Tom Newhouse thinks hand-held telephones that allow global service will be useful in "the 24-hour world of finance and market analysis, where minutes mean millions." And, he adds, "The same can be true for political organizations."

Advancing from in-flight phones to global walkie-talkies won't so much require new technology, our experts confirm, as solving incompatibilities among networks and maintaining connectivity across volatile boundaries. (The first wireless telephone – called the TYK telephone after its inventors, Dr. Torigata Uichi, Yokoyama Eitaro, and Kitamura Seijiro – was first demonstrated in February 1912.)

It is concerning worldwide coordination that Joe Carter lodges his caveat, noting that "the complexities of crossing national borders and dealing with other countries' telecommunication monopolies will be difficult to work out." At best, Carter says, establishing connectivity and smoothing over disagreements among telephone monopolies in various countries will slow the realization of the jet-setter's fantasy of limitless wireless phone access.

URLS FOR FURTHER READING

Eco-8 System: Service focusing on access from remote, tropical regions. www.inpe.be/eco-8.htm INTELSAT: Homepage of the first and largest satellite communications system. www.ece.orst.edu/~dajanis/e478p3.html ORBCOMM: Homepage for a joint venture setting up a global wireless system. www.orbcomm.net/ IRIDIUM – Global Wireless Telecommunications: Homepage to another contender in the race to provide global telecommunication. www.mlb.sticomet.com/sti_irit.htm Global Services – Mobile: Homepage to the installers of the first commercial, national cellular service. cwplc.com

VAN ROMINE, DIRECTOR, INSTITUTE FOR TELEWORK

N. FREDRIC CRANDALL, PH.D., FOUNDING PARTNER, THE CENTER FOR WORKFORCE EFFECTIVENESS, INC.

FRANKLIN D. BECKER, DIRECTOR, INTERNATIONAL WORKPLACE STUDIES PROGRAM, CORNELL UNIVERSITY, AND PARTNER, @WORK CONSULTING GROUP

TOM NEWHOUSE, OWNER/PRINCIPAL, THOMAS J. NEWHOUSE DESIGN, AN INDUSTRIAL DESIGN FIRM

JOE CARTER, MANAGING DIRECTOR, ANDERSEN CONSULTING CENTER FOR STRATEGIC TECHNOLOGY

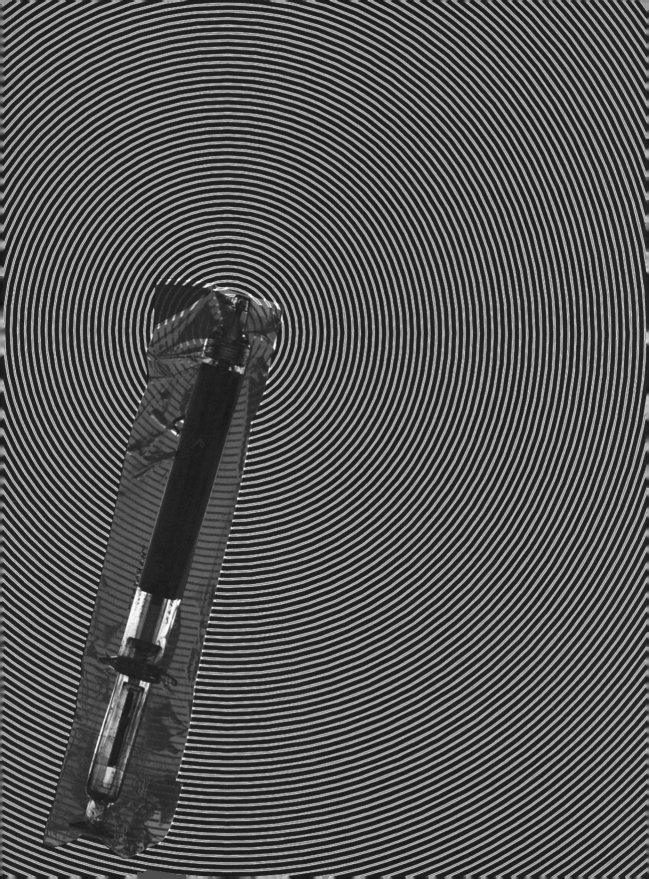

AIDS VACCINE AVAILABLE

2002

Evaluation Working Group of the Office of the AIDS Research Advisory Council: March 1996 report on the National Institute of Health's efforts to investigate and remedy AIDS. www.nih.gov/news/oarreport/evali.html Immune Response Corp: Introduction to a company involved in one of the most advanced clinical trials of an AIDS vaccine. www.sddt.com/files/library/rncorporateprofiles/corpstories/IMMUNERE.html World Health Organization: Homepage of WHO, which tracks AIDS worldwide. www.who.org/ National Council for International Health AIDS Link. www.callamer.com/itc/mindful/vax.html

According to the World Health Organization (WHO), as many as 20 million men, women, and children are infected with human immunodeficiency virus (HIV), the agent believed responsible for AIDS (acquired immune deficiency syndrome). Of the 20 million estimated to have the virus, 4.5 million are reported to have progressed to AIDS, and 2.5 million have died, many in the prime of their lives. With WHO predicting as many as 10,000 new HIV infections each day – a majority of them in developing nations, where preventive measures available in the United States are cost-prohibitive and/or culturally resisted – a preventive AIDS vaccine has never been more urgently needed nor more susceptible to exaggeration and opportunism.

To date, the only effective vaccine tested in animal trials has led to more controversy than certainty. Chimpanzees inoculated with the vaccine developed antibodies to the virus; when their blood was exposed to HIV in test tubes, their antibodies neutralized it. The problem was that the strain of HIV it defeated had been adapted in the lab. As Dr. Pat Fast explains, "Both human volunteers and chimps in vaccine studies have developed antibodies against laboratory strains of HIV, but when less sensitive assays were used with "wild" strains of HIV, antibodies were not detected. It is controversial which antibody test, if either, predicts protection in humans."

These results point to the chief biological challenge for scientists developing an AIDS vaccine: the evolutionary adaptability of HIV. As HIV infection spreads in a person's body, "parent forms" of the virus give rise to a swarm of new HIV, each slightly different than the parent forms. In fact, Dr. David E. R. Sutherland cites the mutability of HIV as the reason we may never see a 100-percent-effective AIDS vaccine. StilÍ, many vaccines are not 100 percent effective.

The National Institute of Allergy and Infectious Diseases (NIAID), which spearheads federal funding of biomedical research on AIDS/HIV for the National Institutes of Health (NIH), reports that to date approximately 36 experimental vaccines have reached various stages of human testing. Dr. Frank Lee has faith that the vaccine the NIAID terms "live attenuated virus vaccine" will be available by 2000. Dr. Cynthia Robbins-Roth suggests that by 2004, a combination of vaccines and boosters will work together to neutralize HIV. "If one of the two vaccine candidates in development right now proves effective, then we could have a vaccine by 2001," says Dr. Fast. "If these are either not tested or not successful, then there is nothing far enough along to say when it might be available." Regardless, she adds, "it's impossible to say for sure."

The single greatest determining factor in expediting the development and distribution of an AIDS vaccine will likely not be science, but money. In the United States, only private corporations can move quickly to fund clinical trials. The only real alternative to this market-driven approach remains federal agencies, but the U.S. government's budget priorities lie elsewhere. As Brenda Lein of Project Inform notes, "The entire budget of the NIH is still less than the cost of one Stealth bomber."

FRANK LEE, PH.D., MOLECULAR BIOLOGIST

DR. PAT FAST, NATIONAL INSTITUTE FOR ALLERGIES AND INFECTIOUS DISEASES*

CYNTHIA ROBBINS-ROTH, PH.D., EDITOR-IN-CHIEF OF BIOVENTURE PUBLISHING, INC.

DR. DAVID E. R. SUTHERLAND, M.D., PH.D., PROFESSOR OF SURGERY AND DIRECTOR OF THE PANCREAS TRANSPLANT PROGRAM, UNIVERSITY OF MINNESOTA

*IF CURRENT CANDIDATE VACCINES PROVE EFFICACIOUS

enjoy her flowers the way sh
used to before this incident
befell us but the conditions
for such a thing are well be
our current paucious means.
Please send whatever you car
as we are in a difficult
situation; there is no one e

Gary

COMPUTER HANDWRITING RECOGNITION

2002

If there's any debate over the technology that enables a person to write longhand (or shorthand) on a computer display and have it flawlessly translated into type, it's not whether it will happen – it's how great a demand it will answer. Robert Jacobson, for one, predicts that only a small segment of the population will ever use such personal digital assistants ("palm tops") to transfer their field notes into WordPerfect files.

As for which devices that recognize handwriting will succeed in the marketplace, John Markoff speaks for most interface experts when he says it will come down to those with "large dictionaries and fast processors." Don Norman breaks down the advances in handwriting recognition this way: for printing in Roman languages, 1996; for reliable cursive in Roman languages, 1999; for printing in Asian and Cyrillic languages, 1998; for cursive in Asian and Cyrillic languages, 2000. But don't tell ParaGraph and FreeStyle about having to wait until 1999 for cursive recognition. These companies claim their products already do it.

personal recognition application for the Newton. www.landware.com/products/freestyleps.html Human Language Technology Project Summary: A helpful introduction to the field by one of its leading commercial research firms. www.cedar.buffalo.edu/Linguistics/summary.html The Unipen Project: Homepage for an electronic writing tablet. www.nici.kun.nl/unipen/welcome.html Handwriting Recognition Group – NICI: Homepage to a Dutch institute. www.nici.kun.nl/handwriting-recognition.html Lexicus Longhand: Software company's homepage. Like visiting an authorized dealer. www.mot.com/MIMS/lexicus/Longhand/index.html

DENISE CARUSO, DIGITAL COMMERCE COLUMNIST FOR *THE NEW YORK TIMES*, AND EXECUTIVE PRODUCER OF THE SPOTLIGHT CONFERENCE ON INTERACTIVE MEDIA

JOHN MARKOFF, REPORTER, *THE NEW YORK TIMES*, AUTHOR OF *CYBERPUNK: OUTLAWS AND HACKERS ON THE COMPUTER FRONTIER*

ROBERT JACOBSON, FOUNDER AND PRESIDENT, WORLDESIGN, INC.

DON NORMAN, VICE PRESIDENT, ADVANCED TECHNOLOGY, APPLE COMPUTER

1988
1989
1990
1991
1992
1993
1994
1995
1996
1997
1998
1999
2000
2001
2002
2003
2004
2005
2006
2007
2008
2009
2010
2011
2012
2013
2014

FAT-DESTROYING PILL

2002

Early in the next century, gym memberships may decline as the weight- and waist-conscious no longer need treadmills to burn off their favorite fast foods. Instead, all that will be required of those wishing to remain thin is to pop a fat-destroying pill.

The prospects for such a pill begin with a current line of over-the-counter products called thermotropics. These "weight control," "weight loss," or "dietary" supplements are generally sold as powders that are added to a blended drink. A couple of the better known brands include Diet Max and Rainbow Light's "Heat Wave." These products accelerate one's metabolic rate and so help the body to burn fats faster – hence their nickname, "fat burners."

Dr. Marc S. Leventhal anticipates improvement in these metabolic fat burners, and says that they may lead to a fat-destroying pill. Leventhal and others, however, qualify their predictions, noting that while an effective weight-loss pill may strike some as a convenient way to keep one's love handles under control, it will not replace the benefits of regular exercise. G. D. Castillo goes further. He thinks a miracle, fat-off pill will probably be effective only for people who have plumped up in the last five years and will prove less effective for long-standing obesity.

CNN – Race Is on for Fat Pill: A new report published by CNN's online business page on advances with leptin, a chemical that has made mice thin. cnn.fn.com/news /9601/08/weight.loss/index.html Zero Fat – Fat Burner: A testimonial endorsement for The Fat Absorber, an "amazing food supplement that absorbs 12 times its weight in fat." www.zerofat.com/absorbitol.html Drink Pink to Shrink: Homepage for an elixir that helps you stay trim. www.doubleclickd.com/ruesch.html Thermolift: Site to learn about a commercial metabolic enhancer. www.altech.ccinet.ab.ca/neil/thermo.htm Health EnhancementR – Thermo-Dynamix: Site to learn about another, commercial metabolic enhancer. nst.netwkcal.com/healthenhancement/healthd.htm

DOUGLAS DEDO, M.D., FACS, ASSISTANT CLINICAL PROFESSOR OF OTOLARYNGOLOGY, HEAD AND NECK SURGERY, UNIVERSITY OF MIAMI MEDICAL SCHOOL

MARC S. LEVENTHAL, M.D., FACS, DIPLOMAT OF THE AMERICAN BOARD OF COSMETIC SURGERY, MEMBER OF EDITORIAL ADVISORY BOARD OF AMERICAN JOURNAL OF COSMETIC SURGERY, AND FORMER BOARD MEMBER OF AACS

STEVEN NATHANSON, M.D., FACS

G. D. CASTILLO, M.D., FACS, PRESIDENT-ELECT OF THE AMERICAN ACADEMY OF COSMETIC SURGEONS (AACS)

1989 1990 1991 1992 1993 1994 1995 1996 1997 1998 1999 2000 2000 2001 **2002** 2003 2004 2005 2006 2007 2008 2009 2010 2011 2012 2013 2014

BOTTOM LINE: WEIGHT LOSS OR CONTROL WILL BECOME AS SIMPLE AS POPPING A PILL BY 2002.

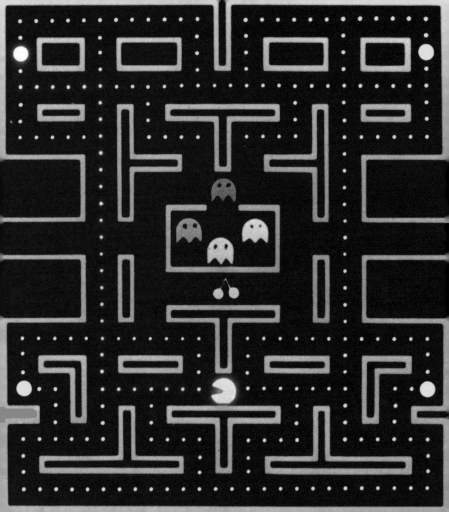

2002

The surgeon, a leader in her field, watches a TV screen in Brussels, her DataGlove-clad hand poised for action. Moving her hand carefully, she observes the video image of a precise incision she makes in her patient – who lies on an operating table in Cape Town, South Africa.

Whether such surgery will ever come to pass is likely less a question of "Can it be done?" than "When, if ever, will it be warranted?" And when would it? Well, say our experts, when eminent surgeons could not be on hand but could make themselves available via telepresence, or if, under battlefield conditions, it's too risky to transport a physician to a wounded soldier. (In fact, one elaborate scenario for remote-controlled battlefield surgery is known in the military as "Doc in a Box." A coffin-sized, self-contained high-tech box would get dropped wherever the fallen soldier lay. Placed inside the box, the soldier would be sealed in and would then undergo telesurgery.)

Far-fetched as all this sounds, (our experts generally don't consider the "Doc in a Box" practical), telesurgery over a closed circuit has already been conducted in Italy (a surgeon operated on a patient in a hospital six miles away), and in most intricate surgeries today surgeons watch their work, magnified, on a TV screen. Thus the leap to telesurgery is not so great.

Dr. Anthony DiGioia thinks that virtual-reality medical technology will be used primarily to enable experts to assist a surgeon from a remote location, but that the physically present surgeon would still do most of the prodecure. Dr. Richard Satava points out that optimally the surgeon and patient will be linked by fiber-optic cable, because with satellites, "the 'lag time' from when you move your hand to when the instrument moves is too great."

All our experts see virtual reality without real patients – animations – as a major learning tool and say that telesurgery's educational promise is what drives this technology.

URLS/FURTHER READING
Cooperative Telesurgery: A prototype for telesurgery under construction at MIT. *web.mit.edu/hmsl/www/markott/cooptelesurg.html* Telepresence Surgery: Cool photos of some state-of-the-art hardware. *os.sri.com/medical/tele_photos.html* TeleMed.Virtual: Surgeons in Cyberspace: Article with discussion of "Doc in a Box." *www.uthscsa.edu/mission/spring94/featu_n.html*

PHILIP GREEN, M.D., PRESIDENT, TELESURGICAL CORPORATION

ANTHONY DIGIOIA III, M.D., CO-DIRECTOR, CENTER FOR MEDICAL ROBOTICS AND COMPUTER-ASSISTED SURGERY, CARNEGIE MELLON UNIVERSITY

DAVID VINING, M.D., ASSISTANT PROFESSOR OF ABDOMINAL IMAGING, BOWMAN-GRAY SCHOOL OF MEDICINE, WAKE FOREST UNIVERSITY

RICHARD SATAVA, M.D., PROGRAM MANAGER, ADVANCED BIOMEDICAL TECHNOLOGY, ADVANCED RESEARCH PROJECTS AGENCY

1988 1989 1990 1991 1992 1993 1994 1995 1996 1997 1998 1999 2000 2001 **2002** 2003 2004 2005 2005 2006 2007 2008 2009 2010 2011 2012 2013

UNIVERSAL PICTURE PHONES

2003

By the time AT&T unveiled the first Picture-phone at the New York World's Fair in 1964, the idea of people conversing face-to-face over a telephone line was well on its way to becoming one of the most anticipated advances of the future. Picture phones, after all, appeared in fiction – Victor Appleton's *Tom Swift and his Photophone* – as early as 1914, and were de rigueur features of televised sci-fi such as *The Jetsons* and *Star Trek*. And yet by 1973, AT&T had abandoned its prototype and would not offer a new videophone for the home market until 1992 – and then at a price out of most budgets – US$1,500.

Meanwhile, software that enables videoconferencing on the desktop – using a fast modem, a digital- or videocamera, and a multimedia-equipped PC – has made inroads with businesses, enabling associates to meet and videoconference rather than travel to meeting locations. In this way, the videophone appears to have arrived, finally, not as a stand-alone device, but as yet another added value of the PC.

Still, promises of start-up packages for less than US$200 not withstanding, our experts note that full-motion videoconferencing has yet to be seen. "Thin pipes" (i.e., old phone lines) and high cost per participant continue to prevent the virtual water cooler from being packaged, like CD-ROMs and modems, with business-use computers. The shift will come, says Van Romine, when "ordering ISDN [a technology that facilitates digital transmission over traditional phone lines] is as easy as getting a burger at your local diner." Others, like Joe Carter, believe that "low bandwidth and shared applications and workspace tools that don't require video may fulfill most collaborative needs as well as or better than video."

As for the impact on our social lives, Derrick de Kerckhove is convinced that videophones will create a massive videophone-sex market (see also "Virtual Sex Slave", page 133), and he facetiously foresees a "short-lived but lively fad, 'video-streaking,' which will involve mooning others via videoconferencing."

URLS/FURTHER READING
Teleview Plus: Homepage for low-cost videoconferencing software. *www.videoconf.com* Teleview Plus Product Information: A site to get you excited about this desk-top videophone software. *www.calypso.com/vcc/product.htm* CU-SeeMe: Videophone company with a successful mnemonic and trial shareware. *www.wpine.com /ins.htm* Telescape Communications, Inc.: Another software option you can download and try. *www.telescape.com/html/products.htm* Desktop Videoconferencing Products: An index of the many videoconferencing products available. *www3.ncsu.edu/dox/video/products.html*

DERRICK DE KERCKHOVE, DIRECTOR OF THE MCLUHAN PROGRAM, THE UNIVERSITY OF TORONTO

VAN ROMINE, DIRECTOR, INSTITUTE FOR TELEWORK

JOE CARTER, MANAGING DIRECTOR, ANDERSEN CONSULTING CENTER FOR STRATEGIC TECHNOLOGY

@WORK CONSULTING GROUP

N. FREDRIC CRANDALL, PH.D., FOUNDING PARTNER, THE CENTER FOR WORKFORCE EFFECTIVENESS, INC.

FRANKLIN D. BECKER, DIRECTOR, INTERNATIONAL WORKPLACE STUDIES PROGRAM, CORNELL UNIVERSITY, AND PARTNER,

TOM NEWHOUSE, OWNER/PRINCIPAL, THOMAS J. NEWHOUSE DESIGN, AN INDUSTRIAL DESIGN FIRM

ONE-FIFTH OF U.S. WORKERS TELECOMMUTE

2003

Here's a concept that has survived even though the reality has – until very recently – lagged well behind the hype: telecommuting. Coined 23 years ago, the term *telecommuting* refers to replacing the conventional commute to work (whether by car or public transit), with telecommunications – telephones, modems, and other desktop computer technologies (see pages 35 and 65, "Universal Picture Phones" and "Fiber to the Home"). Its advantages are nearly as well-known as the term: less air pollution (from car exhaust), "drive time" spent instead with family, and improved worker morale.

Certainly, if businesses are looking for empirical evidence that telecommuting is catching on and is not, as pessimists suggest, counterproductive, they can now find it. According to the University of Maryland, for example, AT&T has 22,500 employees who qualify as full-time telecommuters, and nationwide 9.1 million are reported to be part-time telecommuters. (Though he doesn't doubt these statistics, Tom Newhouse cautions that there's a need to distinguish "telecommuters from those who work at home, like me, and have no other workplace to go to.")

Conferring with a panel of experts on workplace management, we learned that they expect the number of telecommuters to triple in the next 15 years, and that 20 percent of the U.S. workforce will telecommute by 2003. This growth in telecommuting, they say, will be driven by air-quality restrictions, rising demand for adaptability in business (by which they mean employees changing their jobs over time), and improved communications.

Franklin D. Becker says that "a variety of easily accessed telework centers are likely to function as well as or better than an office." N. Fredric Crandall, however, warns that the work-at-home route can lead to a "virtual dead end" characterized by employee isolation and bureaucratic ineffectiveness. "The idea has to be to get people into the field so that they can be more responsive to customers' requirements," Crandall says, "rather than accommodating to their own individual lifestyles."

Haworth Office Journal ▪ Telecommuting: A decent overview of telecommuting, the prophets, and the naysayers. www.haworth.com/haworth/JSA/office/office.htm

Telecommuting Guide: A guide to those new to the concept. smartone.svi.org:80/PROJECTS/TCOMMUTE/TCGUIDE/ Defining A New Workplace: A slightly gee-whiz first pass at the subject. www.att.com/Telecommute_America/discover.html Center for the New West Institute for Telework: Homepage of a Denver-based think tank thoughtful on telecommuting. www.newwest.org/cnw/telework.html Telework: The Trend Towards Networking (Denmark): If this site is any indication, the Danes get telecommuting. www.icbl.hw.ac.uk/telep/resource/LarsTelework.html

JOE CARTER, MANAGING DIRECTOR, ANDERSEN CONSULTING CENTER FOR STRATEGIC TECHNOLOGY

TOM NEWHOUSE, OWNER/PRINCIPAL, THOMAS J. NEWHOUSE DESIGN, AN INDUSTRIAL DESIGN FIRM

VAN ROMINE, DIRECTOR, INSTITUTE FOR TELEWORK

FRANKLIN D. BECKER, DIRECTOR, INTERNATIONAL WORKPLACE STUDIES PROGRAM, CORNELL UNIVERSITY, PARTNER, @WORK CONSULTING GROUP

N. FREDRIC CRANDALL, PH.D., FOUNDING PARTNER, THE CENTER FOR WORKFORCE EFFECTIVENESS, INC.

1996 1997 1998 1999 1999 2000 2001 2002 **2003** 2004 2005 2006 2007 2008 2009 2010 2011 2012 2013 2014 2015 2016 2017 2018 2019 2020 2021

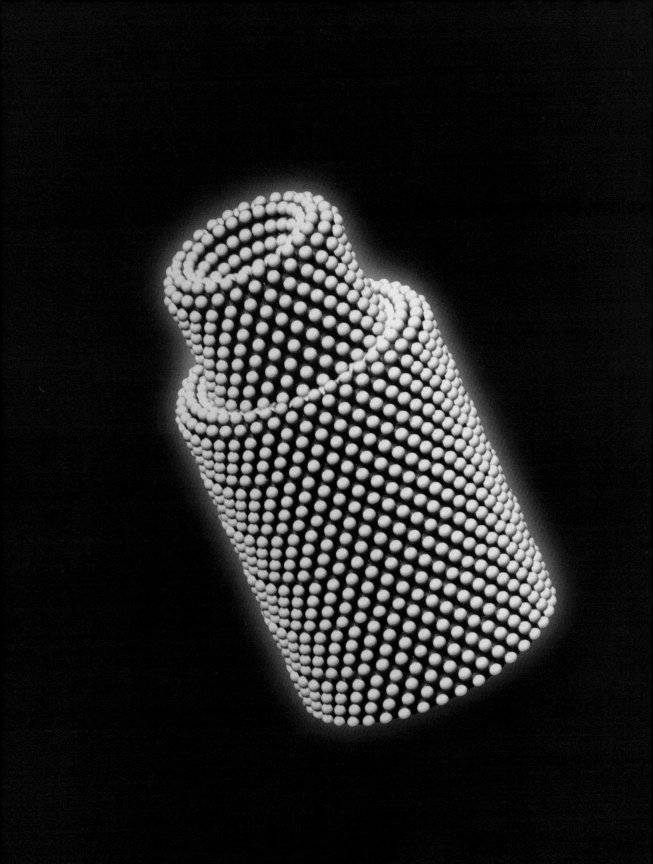

COMMERCIALLY VIABLE NANOTECHNOLOGY

2004

Terabytes of memory and dazzling processing speed from a computer smaller than a pinhead; swarms of microscopic robots that neutralize cancer cells, eat rust for lunch, or reconfigure hard plastic to produce a repeatedly customizable toilet seat; self-replicating molecular machines that "grow" into a product just as growing cells form a mature organism – these are some of the visions, useful and whimsical, that nanotechnology may someday enable. (See also "Cell Repair Technology," page 119, and "Self-Replicating Robot," page 127). But the current reality of nanotechnology is far more prosaic.

Getting at the truth of nanotechnology first requires agreeing on a definition of it. If, for example, one refers to nanotechnology as any activity at the nano scale (one billionth of a meter), then nanotechnology could include ultra-high-resolution lithography. Lines this narrow are feasible today. Ralph C. Merkle of Xerox's Palo Alto Research Center (Xerox PARC), however, contends that the appropriate definition of nanotechnology is "a manufacturing technology able to inexpensively fabricate most structures [in a manner] consistent with natural law, and to do so with molecular precision." In short, nanotechnology is a "bottom-up" approach to engineering, one that builds on the stipulation, expressed by physicist Richard Feynman in a 1959 speech at Caltech, that "the principles of physics, as far as I can see, do not speak against the possibility of maneuvering things atom by atom."

Only the most tentative steps toward creating useful nanotech engineering tools have been made, and most current progress is largely limited to computer simulations. (An advance beyond computer simulation came in 1993, when Mark Veolker, a graduate student at the University of Arizona, developed a specialized microscope that allowed him to move, clumsily, a single atom of carbon.)

What might the first commercially viable nanotechnologic product be? Richard E. Smalley suggests it could be a chemically synthesized biosensor, placed on the tip of a needle, that could first recognize biological agents in the bloodstream or measure blood-sugar levels and then send the information out of the body for analysis. K. Eric Drexler, however, predicts that a first application will occur not in medicine, but in electronics. "A good candidate for the first product to make a big splash," says Drexler, "is a molecular-based computer memory."

1997 defines the term. www.leland.stanford.edu/~jkassis/pub/IDM/idm.definitions.html A response to Scientific American's news story "Trends In Nanotechnology" by Ralph C. Merkle. www.foresight.org/SciAmResponse.html Computational Molecular Nanotechnology at NASA Ames Research Center: NASA's foray into nanotech research

1998 with short- and long-term objectives. www.nas.nasa.gov/NAS/Projects/nanotechnology/ Foresight Institute: With access to Engines of Creation, this is the single best

1999 site to keep track of what's happening in nanotechnology. www.foresight.org/

2000 DONALD W. BRENNER, PH.D., ASSOCIATE PROFESSOR, DEPARTMENT OF MATERIALS SCIENCE AND ENGINEERING, NORTH CAROLINA STATE UNIVERSITY

2000 RICHARD E. SMALLEY, PH.D., PROFESSOR OF CHEMISTRY AND PHYSICS, RICE UNIVERSITY, AND CHIEF INVESTIGATOR OF RICE'S CENTER FOR NANOSCALE SCIENCE AND TECHNOLOGY

2001

2002 ROBERT R. BIRGE, PH.D., DISTINGUISHED PROFESSOR OF CHEMISTRY, AND DIRECTOR OF THE W. M. KECK CENTER FOR MOLECULAR ELECTRONICS, SYRACUSE UNIVERSITY

2003

2004

2005 J. STORRS HALL, PH.D., COMPUTER SCIENTIST, RUTGERS UNIVERSITY, AND MODERATOR, SCI.NANOTECHNOLOGY USENET GROUP

2006

2006

2007

2008

2009

2010

2011

2012

2013

2014

2015 K. ERIC DREXLER, PH.D., CHAIRMAN, FORESIGHT INSTITUTE, AND AUTHOR OF ENGINES OF CREATION: THE COMING ERA OF NANOTECHNOLOGY

2016

2017

2018

2019

2020

2021

SOLAR POWER TO THE PEOPLE

2004

Even though public interest in solar energy has lessened since its peak in the late 1970s, when OPEC was a household acronym, scientists and environmentalists continue to drool over the potential of converting the sun's rays into earth-friendly power. And who could blame them? Every year, approximately 2.5 million exajoules of solar energy reach the earth. That's about 6,000 times the amount of energy consumed annually by the world's population.

What stands between us and the utilization of this abundant, ecologically sound energy, our experts agree, is economic competitiveness. Current solar technology provides power at about 9 cents per kilowatt-hour – a U.S. nickel more than natural gas-generated electricity costs. Actually, today's technology can already produce solar energy at 5 cents per kilowatt-hour, but not on a mass scale, which explains solar energy's popularity in developing nations and with those living "off the grid." Because these users do not require as much energy, they aren't dependent on the vast superstructure needed to concentrate and disseminate solar-generated power and it is this superstructure that drives the cost up.

As for a technical advance that will make solar power cost-competitive for users *on* the grid, Christopher Flavin suggests thin-film solar cells, which, being less than one millimeter thick, are cheaper to manufacture, store, and ship than conventional solar cells. Steven Strong insists that large-scale photovoltaic power plants hold promise, and notes that Enron, a large U.S. natural gas company, has already announced plans for a plant that should lower the price to 5.5 cents per kilowatt-hour. Flavin cautions, however, that the 5.5-cent rate assumes that Enron will receive special tax breaks, and that it will choose to use these savings to offer its customers better electricity rates.

Solar Design Associates, Inc.: Introduction to a leading architecture and engineering firm dedicated to solar energy systems. www.solardesign.com

Utility PhotoVoltaic Group: Homepage for a group that markets photovoltaics. www.ttc/iupvg/INDEX.HTM Solar power means colder power: Article by Tim Thwaites on the Monash group in Australia. www.monash.edu.au/pubs/busvic/BV95_06/solar.html The Village of Lebak: The advantage of solar power for developing nations, explored in Indonesia. solstice.crest.org/renewables/indonesia/lebak.html Solar Electric Power: The advantage of thin film in reducing the cost of solar energy. starfire.ne.uiuc.edu/nezor/webproject/mcconnell/solar5.html

OPERATIONAL SPACE STATION

2004

Images of space stations, positioned in orbit above the blue earth amid the blackness of space, have long floated in popular imagination. Thanks to the likes of Stanley Kubrick, George Lucas, and Steven Spielberg, few among us have trouble imagining moving about inside one. And yet, as they've become easier to picture in the mind's eye, we've become less certain of their purpose.

Most of the literature from NASA's Lewis Research Center, the Russian Space Agency, and the International Space Station Project Office reflects the need to justify this enterprise. A NASA white paper identifying the "6 Reasons Why America Needs the Space Station" considers it "a cutting edge laboratory" in which experiments could be conducted in "microgravity" environments, a "springboard" for global systems management, and an inspiration to America's youth.

Circumstances surrounding one of the rationales NASA cites for a joint U.S.-Russian space station – "a catalyst for international peace and cooperation" – could explain why James Oberg doesn't hold out much hope for a space station's imminence. Oberg predicts that "diplomatic upheavals following Boris Yeltsin's assassination will scuttle the project."

To Timothy Ferris and Lou Friedman, the reasons for a space station must be made clear and should include, in Friedman's words, "preparing and evaluating human adaptability to long-duration missions." Ferris contends that a space station is "a waste of time unless we go to Mars" (see also "Humans on Mars," page 107). These views, at any rate, are roughly consistent with the goals the joint U.S.-Russian project has set for itself: a subscale unit test in 1997, and the launch and operation of two full-scale units beginning in 2002.

Joint U.S.-Russian Solar Dynamic Flight Demonstration: Homepage of this alliance between old Cold War enemies to develop a space station. *godzilla.lerc.nasa.gov/pspo/sddemo.html* International Space Station Size Comparison: Schematics of a space station. *issa-www.jsc.nasa.gov/ss/prgview/sspicts/2D.html* NASA: 6 Reasons Why America Needs the Space Station: White papers and statement of purpose from NASA. *issa-www.jsc.nasa.gov/ss/prgview/sswp.html* The International Space Station: Engineering the Future: The Alpha space station complete with stunning photo and quote from John F. Kennedy. *issa-www.jsc.nasa.gov/ss/prgview/PAO.html*

1996

1997

1998

1999   DAVID MORRISON, CHIEF OF SPACE SCIENCE DIVISION, NASA-AMES RESEARCH CENTER, AND SCIENCE WRITER

2000   LOU FRIEDMAN, EXECUTIVE DIRECTOR, PLANETARY SOCIETY

2001

2002

2003

2004

2005   TIMOTHY FERRIS, AUTHOR OF *THE MIND'S SKY* AND EMERITUS PROFESSOR OF JOURNALISM, UNIVERSITY OF CALIFORNIA, BERKELEY

2006

2007

2008

2009

2010

2011

2012

2013

2014

2015

2016

2017

2018

2019

2020

2021

UNLIKELY   JAMES OBERG, SPACE ENGINEER AND AUTHOR

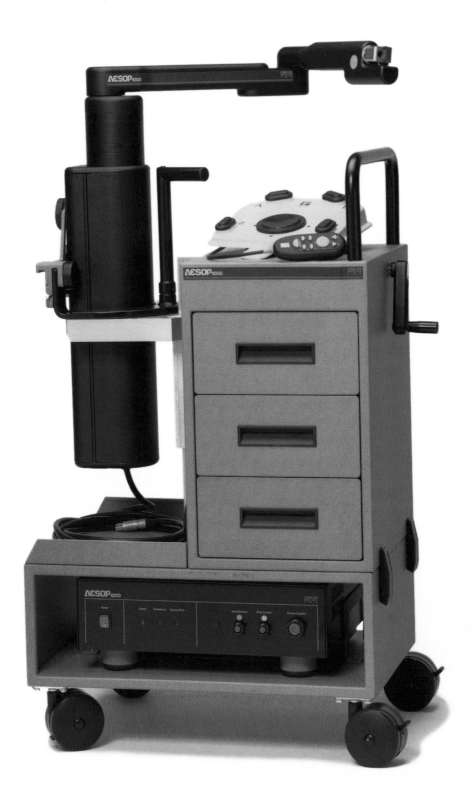

Given that what's often most taxing about a surgical procedure is not rectifying the condition that required the surgery in the first place, but instead trauma to the patient's body and other "complications," surgery that doesn't require patients to go under the knife has obvious appeal.

The experts we consulted agree that the ability to use real-time magnetic resonance imaging (MRI) to watch, say, the destruction of a tumor by high-intensity ultrasound radiation, is only a few years away. While Dr. David Vining expresses concern that ultrasound disintegration of a tumor may cause too much soft-tissue destruc-

tion, Dr. Philip Green comments that clinical results from ultrasound tumor destruction in the human prostate have been encouraging.

Other less invasive developments include a robotic device for endoscopy (a commercial product, AESOP – Automated Endoscopic System for Optimal Positioning – will enter the market at US$20,000 to US$30,000, according to its inventors, Computer Motion, Inc., of Goleta, CA); stereostatic radiosurgery, which enables surgeons to treat small intracranial lesions without drilling a hole in the patient's skull; and several treatments loosely grouped under the category "nuclear medicine and MRI."

To know how and when additional noninvasive surgical techniques will develop, it's best to focus on MRI and other scanning devices, such as holographic medical imaging (see page 47). After all, X-rays, computed tomography (CT), and MRI have reduced by millions the number of exploratory, diagnostic surgeries by providing complete, high-resolution images of the body's interior.

guiding instruments, especially during brain surgery. robotics.jpl.nasa.gov/accomplishments/surgery/surgery.html Current Research in Magnetic Resonance Imaging: The latest research on MRI therapy by radiologists at Brigham and Women's Hospital, Harvard Medical School. www.cfac.uk/uwcm/dr/mirror/BWHRad/HomeDocs /Research/BWHResearchMRI.html AMT: Noninvasive Screening Strain Gauge Plethysmography: An innovative technique for knee and leg injuries. www.unite.net /customers/amt/specification.html

PHILIP GREEN, M.D., PRESIDENT, TELESURGICAL CORPORATION

RICHARD SATAVA, M.D., PROGRAM MANAGER, ADVANCED BIOMEDICAL TECHNOLOGY, ADVANCED RESEARCH PROJECTS AGENCY

ANTHONY DIGIOIA III, M.D., CO-DIRECTOR, CENTER FOR MEDICAL ROBOTICS AND COMPUTER-ASSISTED SURGERY, CARNEGIE MELLON UNIVERSITY

DAVID VINING, M.D., ASSISTANT PROFESSOR OF ABDOMINAL IMAGING, BOWMAN-GRAY SCHOOL OF MEDICINE, WAKE FOREST UNIVERSITY

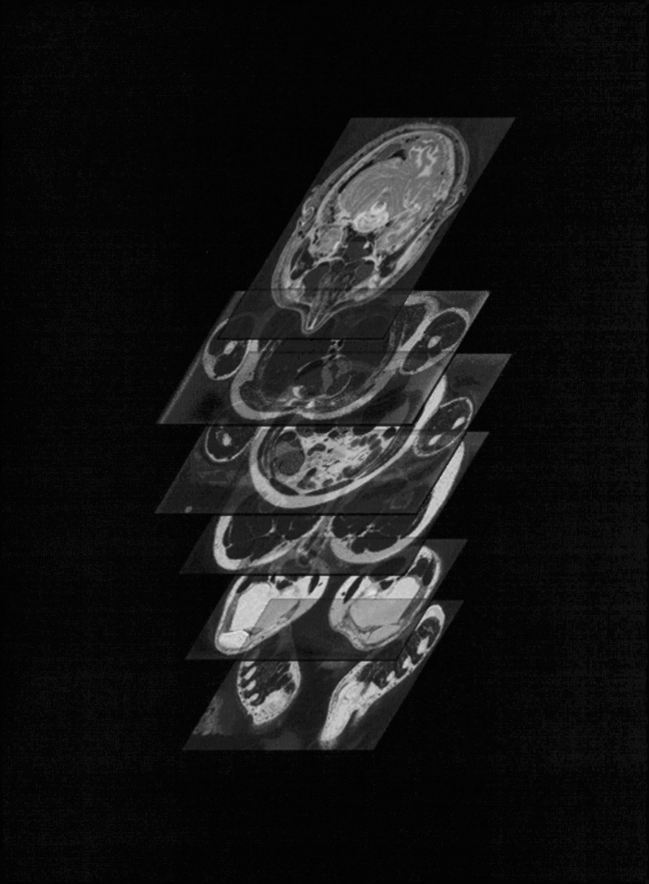

HOLOGRAPHIC MEDICAL IMAGING
2004

The X-ray wall Arnold Schwarzenegger's character walks behind in *Total Recall* left a lasting impression. What if such a technology could actually provide physicians with an instantaneous, full-size map of a patient's bones and soft tissues? Moreover, what if, before operating, a surgeon could examine in 3-D all the organs and tissues in the vicinity of the procedure? Technologies that provide these diagnostic advantages appear within reach, according to some of the pioneers of holographic medical imaging.

At least two technologies have already significantly improved on X-rays: computed tomography (CT) and magnetic resonance imaging (MRI). Now, to make 3-D tissue visualization a reality, engineers are combining the information gathered by CT and MRI scans with the latest in holographic technology.

Stephen A. Benton and Tung Hon Jeong point out that a system produced by Voxel, based in Laguna Hills, CA, has been used in clinical tests to create holograms from both MRIs and CTs. James Fischbach reports a successful trade-show demo in which his firm, American Propylaea, projected a hologram of a human liver several inches in front of a TV monitor so that passers-by could examine the blood vessels at the liver's surface.

Emmett Leith, however, dissents, claiming that many physicians say they don't need this costly technology because they can get the information they need from flat pictures. To this, Mark Diamond replies that holographic medical imaging would still prove useful for teaching, as it could quickly elevate a medical student's acuity to that of a seasoned interpretive radiologist: "You wouldn't have to have 20 years' experience in the field to notice subtleties."

URLS/FURTHER READING

Holography at MIT: A profile of Stephen Benton's spatial imaging group. *alberti.mit.edu/plan/plan/plan4/backup/spatialimaginggr.html* VOXEL: Introduction to work being done by one developer to integrate CT and MRI into one hologram. *www.voxel.com/More/Overview.html#MedImaging* Medical Imaging Analysis: Research opportunities for medical imaging experts. *www.amsta.leeds.ac.uk/Statistics/Statistics/brochure/subsection3_12_4.html* Visualization of 3-D Medical Data by Digital Holography Means: A technical paper reporting on group research in the field. *www.imaging.org/eig6/eig6_2652-08.html*

TUNG HON JEONG, PROFESSOR OF PHYSICS, AND DIRECTOR, THE CENTER OF PHOTONICS STUDIES, LAKE FOREST COLLEGE

JAMES FISCHBACH, PRESIDENT AND CEO, AMERICAN PROPYLAEA, A COMMERCIAL HOLOGRAPHY DEVELOPER

STEPHEN A. BENTON, PH.D., ALLEN PROFESSOR OF MEDIA ARTS AND SCIENCES, SPATIAL IMAGING GROUP, FELLOW, MIT MEDIA LAB

MARK DIAMOND, FOUNDER, DIAMOND IMAGES, INC., AND CREATIVE DIRECTOR AND VICE PRESIDENT, 3-D WORLDWIDE HOLOGRAMS, INC.

EMMETT LEITH, PH.D., PROFESSOR OF ELECTRICAL ENGINEERING AND COMPUTER SCIENCE, UNIVERSITY OF MICHIGAN

1993 1994 1995 1996 1996 1998 2000 2002 **2004** 2006 2008 2010 2012 2014 2016 2018 2020 2022 2024 2026 2028 2030 2032 2034 2036 2038 2040

MOST U.S. PRODUCE GENETICALLY ENGINEERED

2004

The dream of agricultural biotech engineers, as expressed by Carl B. Feldbaum, president of the Biotechnology Industry Organization, is to help produce the food and fiber we need while reducing our reliance on chemical pesticides and herbicides – and without putting additional forests and wildlands under cultivation.

As commendable as that goal sounds, consumers have not taken to initial biotech engineering efforts, such as the "Flavr Savr" tomato. Still, say our experts, this will change. Ellen Martin predicts that "long shelf life will revolutionize produce economics, and good-tasting produce will win customers." Jim McCamant thinks the sea change in attitude toward genetically engineered produce will be its "insect and herbicide resistance." McCamant predicts that when consumers can pay the same for "organic" produce as for conventional produce that has been recently sprayed, the stigma of genetic engineering will fade.

To those wary of biotechnology, Manfred Kroger points out that produce has in fact been genetically engineered for years. Traditional methods of breeding plants to improve yield and quality are nothing if not a form of genetic engineering.

Agbiotech Infosource – Biotechnology and Crops: Explosive population growth means greater and greater demand on crops. A discussion of the problem and some solutions. www.lights.com/agwest/infosource/biotech_crops.html FDA Backgrounder – FLAVRSAVR tomato: Consumer awareness pamphlet published online. www.biotech.wisc.edu/Education/FDABacK.html IFIC Foundation: A useful, if uncritical introduction to argicultural biotechnology. ificinfo.health.org/whatsbio.htm Regulation of Genetically Engineered Organisms and Products: A thorough overview from Iowa State University. www.inform.umd.edu:8080/EdRes/Topic/AgrEnv /Biotech/Education.res/.bion.html

MANFRED KROGER, PH.D., PROFESSOR OF FOOD SCIENCE, PENNSYLVANIA STATE UNIVERSITY

MAHMOUD EL-BEGEARMI, PH.D., NUTRITION AND FOOD SAFETY SPECIALIST, UNIVERSITY OF MAINE COOPERATIVE EXTENSION

ELLEN MARTIN, SCIENCE COMMUNICATIONS, DNA PLANT TECHNOLOGY

JIM McCAMANT, EDITOR, AGBIOTECH STOCK LETTER

1945 1950 1955 1960 1998 1999 2000 2001 2002 2003 **2004** 2005 2006 2007 2008 2009 2010 2011 2012 2013 2014 2015 2016 2017 2018 2020 2030

COMPUTER DEFEATS HUMAN CHESS MASTER

2005

URLS/FURTHER READING
Kasparov vs. Deep Blue: An account of this momentous contest. www.chess.ibm.park.org/ IBM RISC System/6000 – Parallel computing: Info on scalable power computing, the platform for computer chess giants. www.RS.6000.ibm.com/ How People Play Chess (W. Lehnert): An excellent overview and discussion of chess and of chess as a measure of artificial intelligence. www.eksl.cs.umass.edu/~lehnert/79iT/homepage.html A History of Computer Chess. www.to.icl.fi/chess/ai/history.shtml

FREDERIC FRIEDEL, DIRECTOR OF EUROPEAN DEVELOPMENT OF FRITZ, A TOP-RANKED PC-BASED CHESS SYSTEM

MONTY NEWBORN, CHAIR OF THE ACM COMPUTER CHESS COMMITTEE

TONY MARSLAND, PRESIDENT, THE INTERNATIONAL COMPUTER CHESS ASSOCIATON

GARRY KASPAROV, YOUNGEST WORLD CHESS CHAMPION EVER AND FOUR-TIME DEFENDER OF HIS CROWN (2010 OR MAYBE NEVER)

Since 1957, when computer scientist and future Nobel laureate Dr. Herbert Simon predicted that within a decade a computer would be programmed to play chess better than any human, speculation has ebbed and flowed as to when that day would come. It hasn't yet.

A fair number of pundits suggested 1996 might be the year, especially midway through the hotly contested ACM Chess Championship between a computer, "Deep Blue," and defending World Chess Champion Garry Kasparov. Kasparov eventually prevailed, however, prompting him to predict that a computer might be able to best him or another human chess champion in 2010 – or "maybe never."

Speculation on the virtuosity of computer chess programs has stimulated a lively debate. "There is no principled reason that machines should not be able to beat people by a combination of brute force and some clever heuristics," contends Terry Winograd, a computer scientist at Stanford University and co-author, with Fernando Flores, of *Understanding Computers and Cognition*. But, he adds, "I thought from the beginning (the early '70s) [MIT professor and computer scientist] Hubert Dreyfus was barking up the wrong tree in considering chess a means of measuring successful artificial intelligence, rather than as something more rooted in human experience." To this, computer-chess enthusiasts say that creating chess programs is only the beginning, only one complex task that will prove its value many times over in spin-off applications and new technologies. Meanwhile, chess lovers believe that a machine's ultimate success in becoming the world's leading chess player has less to do with computers than with their human rivals. Will young players ardently pursue chess and keep the game at a high level in the future?

To come up with a prediction for the year when a computer would first defeat the reigning world champ, we turned to *Man v Machine, The ACM Chess Challenge: Garry Kasparov v IBM's Deep Blue* by Raymond Keene and Byron Jacobs, published in the U.K. by B. B. Enterprises. In it the authors include a survey of several of the leading authorities on the game of chess and chess as played by computers.

1996 1997 1998 1999 2000 2001 2002 2003 2004 **2005** 2006 2007 2008 2009 2010 2010 2011 2012 2013 2014 2015 2016 2017 2018 2019 2020 2021

UNIVERSAL ORGAN DONOR ANIMAL

2005

Every so often a committee of doctors, nurses, psychologists, and counselors, all trained in medical ethics, assembles within the transplant unit of a hospital to decide who might live and who will die. Who can live the longest before another organ becomes available? Who is most likely to survive the transplant procedure and resume a "normal" life? It's not a conspiracy, it's just the reality they face: several patients need a vital organ transplant, and only one organ is available.

To eliminate the shortage of organs, medical professionals continue to anticipate the day when some nonhuman species, most likely miniature swine (pigs), will supply all the organs needed for human transplants. (*Miniature* is a relative term, as these pigs reach 200–300 lbs.) Dr. David H. Sachs, who has been inbreeding swine for 24 years for just this purpose, says the day will "absolutely" come when organ transplants between swine and humans are possible. (In fact, less complex, but no less essential tissues, such as heart valves, are already transplanted.)

The problem, Sachs and others agree, remains how to prevent the human body from rejecting the substitute organ. To prevent rejection during a transplant, drugs are used to suppress the organ recipient's immune system; currently, recipients' immune systems must be suppressed to the point at which normally routine infections become life-threatening. To build "immune tolerance" of the swine organ in humans, swine are being bred so that they mimic human antigens. (Antigens are proteins that can stimulate an immune response.) Dr. David E. R. Sutherland says that we will have pigs with human antigens within 10 years.

Despite the life-saving motive behind transplantation, several experts contend that ethical and political concerns may ultimately determine the availability of universal organ transplants; one expert suggested that transplants will always be an expensive benefit to a relatively small number of people.

Biotech Companies Set To Profit From Animal-Organ Transplants: Excellent discussion first published in *The Scientist*. www.the-scientist.com/yr1999/oct/transp_991016.html Pig-Human Heart Transplant Breakthrough Claimed: Reuters coverage of Cambridge, UK-based group ready for clinical trials. www.radiology.ucdmc.ucdavis.edu/news/digest/item256_10.html Transgenic Animals: Page that introduces and discusses animals that have genes from other animals. www.lmb.uni-muenchen.de/groups/ibelgaufts/Etransgenic.html Cross-Species Transplants: "At least one man is alive thanks to a pig liver." whyfiles.news.wisc.edu /1097transplant/pigliver.html Human Organ Farms: Concise intro to the field with well-chosen hypertext links. www.scimitar.com/revolution/by_topic/science/pigs.html

FRANK LEE, PH.D., MOLECULAR BIOLOGIST

CYNTHIA ROBBINS-ROTH, PH.D., EDITOR-IN-CHIEF OF BIOVENTURE PUBLISHING, INC.

DR. DAVID E. R. SUTHERLAND, M.D., PH.D., PROFESSOR OF SURGERY AND DIRECTOR OF THE PANCREAS TRANSPLANT PROGRAM, UNIVERSITY OF MINNESOTA

DR. DAVID H. SACHS, PROFESSOR OF SURGERY, HARVARD UNIVERSITY, DIRECTOR OF TRANSPLANTATION, MASSACHUSETTS GENERAL HOSPITAL

1995 1996 1997 1998 1999 2000 2001 2002 2003 2004 **2005** 2006 2007 2008 2009 2010 2011 2012 2013 2014 2015 2016 2017 2018 2019 2020 2020

AY NOT YET

MATURE DEATH

HOUSECLEANING ROBOT

2005

Remember Rosie, the Jetsons' trusty mechanical domestic? Our experts predict that housecleaning robots capable of doing the tasks you hate most may be commercially available within a decade. They disagree, however, on whether or not they will resemble Rosie.

If John Canny is correct, we won't have anthropomorphic vacuum cleaners, but instead "a fleet of mouse- or cockroach-sized robots scurrying around the floor," efficiently sucking up dirt or emitting static electricity to become dust magnets. On the other hand, Joe Engelberger reports that his company has already conducted a large-scale study of a mobile, articulated two-armed robot that could soon (given three more years of substantial R & D funding), be ready to clean house. Beyond tidying up, he says, the machine could be utilized as an "elder-care robot to extend independent living for cognizant but mobility-impaired senior citizens."

As is the case with the even more advanced robots now in development (see "C-3PO Becomes a Reality," page 129), housecleaning robots will have to feature substantially advanced navigation capabilities and significantly improved interfaces before people feel comfortable around them and entrust them with their homes. As Isaac Asimov insisted years ago in his Three Laws of Robotics (first stated in his 1942 story, "Runaround"), robots will have to "serve humans without harming them."

work-in-progress: a cleaning system for hard to reach windows. www.ncl.ac.uk/~neee/Robotics/arcow.html Stanford News, Robot Assistants: Stanford roboticist Oussama Khatib and his update of "Romeo and Juliet." www-leland.stanford.edu/dept/news/relayed/960130orobotassts.html Mobile Robot Research at the MIT AI Laboratory: Veteran and new robots currently being put through the paces at MIT. www.ai.mit.edu/projects/mobile-robots/ Fred & Ginger – Co-Operant Mobile Robotics: University of Salford researchers introduce "Fred" and "Ginger," but not Rosie. www.salford.ac.uk/docs/depts/eee/ffandg.html

RODNEY A. BROOKS, ASSOCIATE DIRECTOR, MIT ARTIFICIAL INTELLIGENCE LABORATORY, AND CHAIR, IS ROBOTICS, INC.

JOE ENGELBERGER, CHAIR, HELPMATE ROBOTICS, INC.

TOSHIO FUKUDA, PROFESSOR OF MICROSYSTEM ENGINEERING AND MECHANO-INFORMATICS, NAGOYA UNIVERSITY, JAPAN

JOHN CANNY, ASSOCIATE PROFESSOR OF COMPUTER SCIENCE, UNIVERSITY OF CALIFORNIA, BERKELEY

RICHARD S. WALLACE, PROFESSOR OF ELECTRICAL ENGINEERING AND COMPUTER SCIENCE, LEHIGH UNIVERSITY

1995 1996 1997 1998 1999 2000 2001 2002 2003 2004 **2005** 2006 2007 2008 2009 2010 2011 2012 2013 2014 2015 2016 2017 2018 2019 2020 2025

TILITY/SOFTWARE DI

ED ON YEARLY SUBSCRIPTION TO HOME/LIFEWARE**********
WITH BILLING PERIODS BEGINNING ON 09/15/05, RATES REFLECT
DIRECT PAYMENT DISCOUNT***********YOUR NEXT SCHEDULED
IS 01/02/05**********DON'T FORGET SOFTWARE SANTA! THIS
SEASON GIVE THE GIFT OF SOFTWARE, WITHOUT LOGGING OUT!!!

	Billing Dates	
	From	To
	03/28/05	05/24/05

.l.l..lll..l..ll.l..ll.l..lll..lll

L N. AGE
4 SPECTERAL AVE.
RKELEY CA 94707

	AMOUNT
34 SPECTERAL AVE.	$152.13
RKELEY CA 94707	$152.13

REVIOUS CHARGES AND CREDITS

REVIOUS AMOUNT DUE	31.15
PAYMENT	12.55
THANK YOU	41.19

	AMOUNT
SMARTHOMEY™	2.95
SMARTGARAGE™	2.95
THE 24 HOUR GARDEN™	2.95
	2.9
MOVIESNET	2.9
03/30 11:12 PM DAWN OF THE DEAD	3.9
04/01 05:12 PM BLADE RUNNER	
04/09 09:18 PM THE PRODUCERS	
04/15 09:41 PM BRAZIL	3.
05/23 12:18 AM THE DAY THE EARTH STOOD STILL	8.
04/30 9:15 PM HEAVY INTO JEFF	7
	39
EUDORA 8.0.2	
WINDOWS 7.2.1	
NETSCAPE 6.2.5	
DAILY MYOPIA NEWS	

Please Pay This Amount Now

SOFTWARE SUPERDISTRIBUTION

2005

The idea behind software superdistribution is actually rather simple: in an age when copying software has become so easy that piracy is rampant, why not charge software users not for acquiring software, but for each time they use it? Or, from a businessperson's point of view, why not make software's ease of replication an advantage rather than a liability?

This new business model, first introduced by Ryoichi Mori of the Japan Electronics Industry Development Association in 1987, works as follows: When a software business develops a useful software product, it actively encourages its free distribution, much as America Online has done with its modem software kit. But the software is useless on computers that do not have a special chip – in effect a special key and a meter – that not only enables the user to run the program, but also informs the software company that its application is in use. Based on the information this chip provides, the company can bill the user, just as utilities and long-distance phone companies do now.

In Mori's prototype, according to the Coalition for Electronic Markets' founder, Brad Cox, "these extra services are provided by a silicon chip that plugs into a standardized slot. The hardware is surprisingly simple – its complexities relate more to providing tamperproofing than to performing its basic function – and is far less compli-cated than hardware the computer industry has been routinely building for years."

Most of our experts expect this "chip" (or other hardware required for superdistribution) to be installed in most PCs by the end of the decade. But superdistribution is not without its naysayers. Curtis Yarvin, for one, finds it hard to believe that computer owners will willingly pay extra for hardware that restricts their ability to copy software. Danny Hillis goes even further, predicting that the development of common software applications such as word processors will be so easy by the turn of the century that a "great software price collapse" will cause "people to pay you to use their software."

URLS/FURTHER READING

Superdistribution: The Concept and the Architecture. www.virtualschool.edu/mon/ElectronicProperty/MoriSuperdist.html Future of Information Commerce.
www.virtualschool.edu/mon/ElectronicProperty/NCRIInfoCommerce.html Intellectual Property Protection: An attorney considers intellectual property online.
blake.oit.unc.edu/copyright.html What if there is a Silver Bullet and the competition gets it first? www.virtualschool.edu/mon/Cox/CoxWhatIfSilverBullet.html

DEREK LEEBAERT, ADJUNCT PROFESSOR, GRADUATE SCHOOL OF BUSINESS, GEORGETOWN UNIVERSITY, AND EDITOR, *THE FUTURE OF SOFTWARE*

1993
1994
1995
1996
1997
1998
1999
2000
2001
2002
2003
2004
2005 SCOTT BROWN, MANAGER, ADVANCED FILE SYSTEMS, NOVELL, INC.
2006
2007
2008
2009
2010 RICHARD MARK SOLEY, VICE PRESIDENT AND TECHNICAL DIRECTOR, OBJECT MANAGEMENT GROUP, INC.
2010 DAVID VASKEVITCH, DIRECTOR OF ENTERPRISE COMPUTING, MICROSOFT CORPORATION
2011
2012
2013
2014
2015
2016
UNLIKELY DANNY HILLIS, FOUNDER, THINKING MACHINES CORPORATION
UNLIKELY CURTIS YARVIN, LANGUAGE ARCHITECT, XAOS TOOLS, INC.

Bidets. Squat toilets. Heated toilet seats. Zero-gravity toilets. Home medical-care toilets that test bodily waste and transmit results to a doctor via modem. Even though these variations and new loo technologies have become available, the North American bathroom hasn't changed a great deal since the modern flush toilet was invented more than 100 years ago.

For the most part, bathroom style varies greatly over regions and cultures, and as anyone who lives with someone who chronically leaves the toilet seat up will tell you, old habits are hard to break. "Being a European," Gianfranco Zaccai says of bidets, "it has always amazed me that the same people who will wash their hands after going to the bathroom are perfectly comfortable using just a piece of paper in other areas." Meanwhile, squat toilets, popular throughout Asia, get a mixed reception from Westerners. While their proponents argue that hovering over the hole is better for the circulation and the back, Newbold Warden believes that "the squatting position significantly compresses the midsection of the body, impeding the elimination of waste." Says Alexander Kira, "The biggest problem with squat toilets is clothing management."

One improvement with near-universal appeal is the automatic flush, self-cleaning toilet, but a survey of lavatory visionaries revealed that housecleaners will remain acquainted with the Ty-D-Bol Man for a while yet. Even though toilets that rinse themselves after each use are making their way into restrooms in gas stations, airports, and other public facilities, it will likely take 10 to 20 years for self-cleaning units to catch on at home.

Limiting factors in their design include the need for water conservation features. Nick Geragi notes that it's difficult to minimize water use in self-cleaning toilets, but Newbold Warden says there are ways to conserve water and points out that his company already produces an antibacterial tile that kills some kinds of germs. Also on the market are sanitizing features such as auto-flush and automatic seat-cover changers, but for the time being, as Mary Jo Peterson points out, "Elbow grease is still required to maintain a toilet."

ProMatura: Research and marketing firm looks at products and services for the "mature market." www.webcom.com/whipcomm/promatura/ After the Great Hanshin Earthquake: The condition of public toilet facilities in Kobe and ensuing problems. www.kobe-cufs.ac.jp/kobe-city/information/cityOffice/toilet.html Clivus Multrum: Homepage for a company that makes a waterless composting toilet in Australia. www.netprophet.co.nz/qld/clivus.htm How a Toilet Works: Color diagrams, straight-forward explanation for the curious, clueless, or emergency plumber. www.stock-info.com/toiworks.htm

NEWBOLD WARDEN, MARKETING SUPERVISOR, TOTO KIKI USA, INC.

MARGARET WYLDE, PH.D., PRESIDENT OF PROMATURA GROUP, AND CO-AUTHOR OF *BUILDING FOR A LIFETIME*

METAFORM PERSONAL HYGIENE SYSTEM

GIANFRANCO ZACCAI, PRESIDENT OF DESIGN CONTINUUM, INC., AND DEVELOPER,

MARY JO PETERSON, CERTIFIED BATHROOM AND KITCHEN DESIGNER

ALEXANDER KIRA, PROFESSOR OF ARCHITECTURE, CORNELL UNIVERSITY, AND AUTHOR OF *THE BATHROOM*

NICK GERAGI, DIRECTOR OF EDUCATION, NATIONAL KITCHEN AND BATH ASSOCIATION

1991
1992
1993
1994
1995
1996
1997
1998
1999
2000
2001
2002
2003
2004
2005
2006
2007
2008
2009
2010
2011
2012
2013
2014
2015
2025
UNLIKELY

G. D. CASTILLO, M.D., FACS, PRESIDENT-ELECT OF THE AMERICAN ACADEMY OF COSMETIC SURGEONS (AACS)

DOUGLAS DEDO, M.D., FACS, ASSISTANT CLINICAL PROFESSOR OF OTOLARYNGOLOGY, HEAD AND NECK SURGERY, UNIVERSITY OF MIAMI MEDICAL SCHOOL

STEVEN NATHANSON, M.D., FACS

MARC S. LEVENTHAL, M.D., FACS, DIPLOMAT OF THE AMERICAN BOARD OF COSMETIC SURGERY, MEMBER OF EDITORIAL ADVISORY BOARD OF AMERICAN JOURNAL OF COSMETIC SURGERY

2000
2001
2002
2003
2004
2005
2006
2006
2007
2008
2009
2010
2011
2012
2013
2014
2015
2016
2017
2018
2019
2020
2021
2022
2023
2024
2025

Ads for shampoos that thicken hair and fertilize barren scalps still clutter the sports pages, and infomercials still chronicle the "before and after" wonders of formulas with minoxidil and similar agents. Listening to their claims, you'd think baldness had become optional. Still, even though such treatments have been known to mitigate forehead expansion, male pattern baldness continues, same as it ever was.

To men hoping that baldness will not be a feature of middle age, our experts are encouraging. Although they tend to dismiss the formulas in all the ads, they see promise in genetic engineering, noting that male pattern baldness is less a function of hygiene than a genetic trait.

Douglas Dedo, for one, believes that if your grandfather has a shiny dome, the best way to prevent baldness later in life may be to genetically engineer your DNA to stimulate hair follicles to continue pumping out strands.

Even though some of the gene-splicing technology and know-how this scenario requires are practiced in labs today, our panelists think other benchmarks in biotechnology and genetic research will have to come first. Even then, the medical community will have to work hard to prove it really knows what it is doing if it is to reduce people's anxiety over returning altered genes to their bodies.

Meanwhile, notes G. D. Castillo, if you're already in need of a toupee, no geneticist can bring back locks that are already gone.

ONE-FOURTH OF U.S. HOMES GET SMART

2006

Smart homes have been such a regular feature of the future that their arrival is almost a cliché. Certainly, Hollywood has gotten plenty of footage out of the capabilities of high-end automated security systems, outfitting James Bond villains, for example, with some of the more elaborate building-defense mechanisms. Now that some of the technology is becoming widely available, marketers are making matters worse, clouding the concept by referring to such services as integrated services digital network phone lines (ISDN; see "Fiber to the Home," page 65) as smart-home technologies.

At least for our purposes here, a "smart home" is one in which any number of mundane tasks are automated and managed by a computer. The trademarked Smart House, for instance, has more than 25 discrete features, from automatic operation of appliances and sprinkler systems, to motion controls that turn lights on and off as you enter or exit a room, to temperature-control systems that adjust the heat so the house is warm when you rise, cool when you're away, and always economical.

Today, a few thousand homes qualify as smart homes, although millions more have a timer on the coffee pot – qualifying them, perhaps, as smart homes with very low IQs. By 2006, say designers and builders of smart residences, 25 percent of U.S. homes will have some automation technology installed, and many will include programmability from a console in the basement or a desktop in the den, using a PC to micromanage the indoor environment.

Several factors, our experts say, will speed the acceptance of home automation: (1) investment from large corporations that can mass-produce the components and thus lower their price, which is already happening; (2) digital wiring, which will enable the automated services to be more easily integrated; (3) usefulness for disabled persons; (4) local, state, and federal environmental-protection ordinances, which will limit or make illegal wood-burning fireplaces and stoves, making programmable natural-gas-burning fixtures more attractive; and (5) fear, because security systems may get a lot of home-automation systems in the door.

"Right now [home automation] is laborious, very difficult to coordinate, and temperamental," warns Katherine Lambert, "and if something goes wrong you can begin to feel like your house is an enemy." A lot of home buyers, she says, may be eager to save on their utility bill and prepared to have their lights dim on cue, but not without familiar, manual overrides such as wall switches.

Management System: A home management module introduced with links to support, feedback and even jobs in smart home sales. www.amp.com/product /smart_hs.html Future Homes – The New Smart House Systems: Online newsletter, Cyberhome magazine. 207.55.5.1.80/cyberhome www.real-world.com/cyberhome/homeauto/haz.html Smart House User Interaction. dir.mcc.ac.uk/~perdita/Work/Projects/shui.html Tomorrow's Smart House Is Here Today: Overview of smart home technology, circa 1991, excerpted from Energy & Environmental News. cayuga.nfesc.navy.mil/energy/neesa/smarths.htm

MARK LOCKAREFF, DIRECTOR OF BUSINESS DEVELOPMENT, ECHELON CORPORATION

REZA RAJA, APPLICATIONS ENGINEER, ECHELON CORPORATION

ED ABELITE, PRESIDENT, MILLENNIUM HOMES

KATHARINE LAMBERT, PRINCIPAL PARTNER AND ARCHITECT, FACE ARCHITECTS

"FIBER TO THE HOME"

2007

Movies as picture-perfect as any delivered by cable TV or satellite today, but available over the Net; Web browsing and downloading capabilities that function as quickly as you do; PC-based videoconferencing without the delay between the audio and visual signals that gives present-day videoconferences the look of a badly dubbed foreign film – for these technical advances to become reality, more bandwidth is needed, and station-to-station "fiber to the home" continues to be the vogue catchphrase for the solution.

"Fiber" in this case refers to fiber-optic cable (as opposed to the coaxial cable of cable TV), and MIT Media Lab's Nicholas Negroponte, for one, thinks generations to come will curse us for a lack of foresight if we don't use it to close the circuit between ourselves and the Net. Others, however, debate whether fiber optics are really necessary for a majority of consumers. Instead of rewiring exclusively with fiber-optic lines, they envision "fiber to the curb" (to a neighborhood or block), with the last stage of transmission occurring over "twisted pair" (industry-speak for conventional copper telephone lines) – or, as Derrick de Kerckhove suggests, going wireless. Mostly, our experts place their bets on cable modems, now being tested, that could take advantage of coaxial cables already in place, to link with and communicate over the Net.

"The notion of 'fiber to the home,'" summarizes John Bringenberg, "was always a telco [telephone company] buzz – born, I believe, of a rate-based, PUC [public utilities commission] business model. In fact, what people want is 'bandwidth to the home,' which exists and is available to over 90 percent of homes in the United States through cable TV. Getting the plant conditioned for two-way and using digital modems and data streams will unleash this broadband capability, and the world will never be the same."

& Electro-Optics Research Center: Homepage to the largest educational fiber optics group. www.eevt.edu/ee/research/fiber.html Fiber Optic Technologies, Inc.: Why this corporation thinks it deserves your business and investment. www.teleport.com/~fottrain/ 3Com Impact ISDN External Digital Modem: Introducing the ISDN modem with all of its merits in bullet point. www.anixter.com/impact.html Tele-Communications, Inc.: Homepage to the corporate giant building the Internet's infrastructure for the public and profit. www.tcinc.com/

MICHAEL SCHARGE, MIT MEDIA LAB FELLOW AND CONTRIBUTING EDITOR FOR I.D MAGAZINE

MAURICE WELSH, DIRECTOR OF NEW MEDIA MARKET DEVELOPMENT, PACIFIC BELL

BENJAMIN BRITTON, ASSISTANT PROFESSOR AT THE UNIVERSITY OF CINCINNATI'S COLLEGE OF DESIGN, ART, ARCHITECTURE AND PLANNING

DERRICK DE KERCKHOVE, DIRECTOR OF THE MCLUHAN PROGRAM, THE UNIVERSITY OF TORONTO

JOHN BRINGENBERG, DIRECTOR OF BUSINESS DEVELOPMENT, TELE-COMMUNICATIONS, INC.

SMART FABRICS GO MAINSTREAM

2007

Concepts for "smart fabrics" – materials that automatically adjust to their environment – range from those that change colors to indicate the presence of airborne pollutants, to gloves that function like a cellular telephone (a speaker/mouthpiece and mini-keypad sewn into the cloth), to fabrics that "sing," to fabrics that serve as a computer screen for those who find laptops too bulky.

Well before clothes have RAM or come anywhere near replacing our laptops, we can expect, from sports clothiers, materials that react to both the athlete's temperature and the ambient temperature as well. Fabrics with threads that thicken or knit themselves closer together to close out a chilling breeze, loosen to improve ventilation. The reason these advances will arrive first in athletic apparel, says Haysun Hahn, is that athletes, more than anyone else, demand "performance" from their attire. Ingrid Johnson thinks temperature-sensitive smart fabrics will remain a niche market item, as an all-season outfit would satisfy neither our cultural preference nor the fashion industry's demand for variety in apparel. Jud Early agrees: "Who wants to wear the same thing all year?"

Likewise, our experts are skeptical about a variety of other schemes for adding functionality to clothes. Other innovations in fabric – such as fabrics that improve on denim and leather as protection for bikers against road rash – are good ideas but not "smart" because the fabrics themselves don't adjust to the environment. Pointing, for example, to trendy T-shirts that change color with changes in body heat, our experts predict that the wealth of experiments in smart textiles will generate more fads than lasting, practical clothes.

URLS/FURTHER READING

Clothing Fabric Information: All the various grades of Gore-Tex defined. *www.webspot.com.au/hs/paddypal/fabric.html* **Chameleon Clothing: Learn about the virtues of this temperature sensitive, polychromatic T-shirt.** *www.chameleonwear.com/#whatis* **Campmor Clothing Fabrics: Catalog with ordering info.** *www.campmor.com /clothing/underwear/fabrics.html* **Gore: Homepage to the company that manufactures Gore-Tex fabrics.** *www.gorefabrics.html/index.html* **Rayon – The Multi-Faceted Fiber: Ohio State University fact sheet on rayon fabric, written by Joyce C. Smith.** *www.ag.ohio-state.edu/~ohioline/hyg-fact/5000/5538.html*

1997
1998
1999
2000 MARTHA HARKEY AND GARY HENDERSON, FOUNDERS, YANG SNOWBOARD CLOTHING, INC.
2001
2002
2003
2004
2005 SUNG PARK, PRESIDENT, CUSTOM CLOTHING TECHNOLOGY CORP.
2006
2007
2008
2009
2010 HAYSUN HAHN, DIRECTOR, BUREAU DE STYLE, A TREND FORECASTING COMPANY
2011
2012
2013
2014
2015
2016
2017
2018
2019
2020
2021
UNLIKELY INGRID JOHNSON, CHAIR OF THE TEXTILE DEVELOPMENT AND MARKETING DEPARTMENT, FASHION INSTITUTE OF TECHNOLOGY
UNLIKELY JUD EARLY, DIRECTOR OF RESEARCH AND DEVELOPMENT, TEXTILE/CLOTHING TECHNOLOGY CORP.

ONLINE MASS RETAILER AS BIG AS SEARS

2007

The establishment of a Sears-caliber retailer online, our experts suggest, is less a question of technology than of consumers' habits. Whether there is ever a virtual Sears rests not on the widespread implementation of digital cash (see "E-Cash Gets Real," p. 9), but rather on whether consumers will go online to shop, and on whether they will favor a central location for their shopping needs on the notoriously decentralized Internet.

In conferring with some experts on retail, we didn't find consensus. Steven J. Johnson and Fred Schneider predict that the low costs of entering the online shopping business will create a competitive marketplace, but the market won't support giant one-stop shops as well as it does the little guys. Stuart Spiegel agrees that "the quintessential online merchants will not be general merchants, but mega-niche retailers whose influence transcends their volume potential."

Eric K. Clemons, however, dissents, believing that 10 years from now an electronic shopping mall – home to a wide range of online merchants, all under one virtual roof – will achieve the sales and market power of a department store like Sears. In fact, cyber-malls – Web-based directories of several retailers on a single homepage – already exist.

In sum, it comes down to this: by every indication, Web commerce will improve. According to Mary Modahl of *The Forrester Report on People and Technology*, the Web will represent US$7 billion in activity by 2000, which means that online retail as a whole will surpass Sears. But online commerce will not likely resemble shopping at Sears, where there's a bit of everything in one locale. Nor will it eliminate shopping in person or from mail-order catalogs. After all, as Modahl notes, "Seven billion dollars is diddly when we're talking retail sales. Total retail sales in the United States are more like $5 trillion, and catalog sales total $53 billion."

URLS/FURTHER READING

CUC International: Major financial service provider to more than 30 million members. netmarket.com/nm/pages/cuc/sid=je6f8lB6xv The Internet Business Journal: Article by editor Anuerin Bosley, circa 1994, that covers "Internet Shopping and the Death of Retail." www.phoenix.ca/sie/shopping.html Andersen Consulting – Virtual Smart Store: Site that functions like an online bargain hunter/market research kiosk. smartstore.ac.com/smartstore/ QVC: Web site for the leading shopping network on TV. www.qvc.com/ IN Cybermall: Example of a virtual mall which brings several proprietors together under one URL awning. www.gate.net/~inet/

JOHN D. BENJAMIN, PROFESSOR, DEPARTMENT OF FINANCE AND REAL ESTATE, KOGOD COLLEGE OF BUSINESS ADMINISTRATION, THE AMERICAN UNIVERSITY

ERIC K. CLEMONS, PROFESSOR OF OPERATIONS AND INFORMATION MANAGEMENT, THE WHARTON SCHOOL, UNIVERSITY OF PENNSYLVANIA

RICHARD FERNANDES, EXECUTIVE VICE PRESIDENT OF INTERACTIVE SERVICES, CUC INTERNATIONAL

STEVEN J. JOHNSON, MANAGING PARTNER FOR CONSUMER PRODUCTS, ANDERSEN CONSULTING

FRED SCHNEIDER, EXECUTIVE DIRECTOR OF SMART STORE, ANDERSEN CONSULTING'S R & D CENTER FOR THE FOOD AND PACKAGED GOODS INDUSTRY

STUART SPIEGEL, VICE PRESIDENT AND GENERAL MANAGER OF INTERACTIVE SHOPPING AT QVC

1995 1996 1997 1998 1999 2000 2001 2002 2003 2004 2005 2006 **2007** 2008 2009 2010 2011 2012 2013 2014 2015 2016 2017 2018 UNLIKELY UNLIKELY UNLIKELY

HEMP

BS 7070 Premiu

2008

Even though prohibitions against the growing and harvesting of marijuana have kept hemp products from taking root in the United States, the experts we surveyed believe the ban will soon be lifted, and agree the crop could be processed into an environmentally friendly ethanol-based automobile fuel.

Whether this comes to pass, however, depends both on the market for hemp, (hemp oil has great economic potential in a variety of health, beauty, and industrial applications) and advances in other alternative power sources for cars.

Says John Roulac, "The problem lies in developing technology for making affordable plant-based fuels," not in whether hemp specifically will do the trick. Yet according to Ken Friedman, by the time this technology is developed and efficient, solar-powered or electric autos may have negated the demand for a hemp-based fuel (see also "More than 50 Percent Drive Electric Cars," page 121).

Hemp For Fuel: An archive of information on industrial hemp with links to the latest legal initiatives. *www.forms.com/curiosity/hemp/* The Coalition for Hemp Awareness: Excellent introduction to hemp and hemp activism. *www.indirect.com/www/chaptrk/chat.html* Kentucky Hemp Growers Cooperative Association, Inc.: The story of Kentucky growers of hemp are in this page's links. *pressenter.pressenter.com/~davewest/KYHmpnews.htm* The Industrial Hemp Information Network: Excellent resource for those who grow industrial hemp. *www.west.net/~hemptech/hdir.html* American Hemp Mercantile Incorporated: A catalog of services and materials helpful to hemp farmers. *www.betterworld.com/ahm/home.htm*

CHRISTIE BOHLING, CEO, THE COALITION FOR HEMP AWARENESS, AND A FOUNDER OF HEMP INDUSTRIES

JOHN W. ROULAC, PRESIDENT AND FOUNDER, HEMPTECH, AND EDITOR AND PUBLISHER, *INDUSTRIAL HEMP: PRACTICAL PRODUCTS – PAPER TO FABRIC TO COSMETICS*

KEN FRIEDMAN, PRESIDENT, AMERICAN HEMP MERCANTILE, INC.

JOSEPH W. HICKEY, SR., EXECUTIVE DIRECTOR, KENTUCKY HEMP GROWERS COOPERATIVE ASSOCIATION, INC.

ERWIN A. SHOLTS, DIRECTOR, AGRICULTURAL DEVELOPMENT AND DIVERSIFICATION PROGRAM, WISCONSIN DEPARTMENT OF AGRICULTURE, TRADE, AND CONSUMER PROTECTION

1995 1996 1997 1998 1999 2000 2001 2002 2003 2004 2005 2006 2007 **2008** 2009 2010 2011 2012 2013 2014 2015 2016 2017 2018 2019 2020

BOTTOM LINE: HEMP-BASED AUTO FUEL WILL BE AVAILABLE BY 2008 BUT MAY LOSE OUT TO SOLAR OR ELECTRIC POWER AS THE ENVIRONMENTALLY CORRECT

Beat Supermarket prices. Save up to $2,000 a year

Welcome to the Web Page of the Largest Discount Food Delivery service in Northern California.

Supplying meat and groceries to families since 1958, Blue Ribbon Prime Foods offers a very wide range of first class products without a first class price. Famous name brand groceries delivered right to your home at below supermarket prices, without a delivery charge. Our customers shop in person, or by phone or FAX.

Free Home Delivery!
No Membership Fees!
No Hidden Costs!
America's Finest Meats and Groceries!
No more standing in lines!
And no more pushing carts!

- A sampling of Blue Ribbon's products
- Areas of service
- Find out more about Blue Ribbon Foods

Armour Premium Sliced Bacon 1 LB. PKG. 69¢

Gerber First Foods Baby Food 2.5 OZ. 10¢

Coca-Cola 12 Pack $1.79

SKIPPY Peanut Butter 12 oz. 39¢

20 PERCENT OF U.S. CONSUMERS
TELEGROCERY SHOP
2008

URLS/FURTHER READING
Peapod: "Smart shopping for busy people." Page for info on one of the first and best-known online grocery services. *www.peapod.com/* Kroger: They claim to be the "first supermarket on the Internet." *foodcoop.com:80/kroger/* Smart-Food Co-op: They also claim to be the "first supermarket on the Internet." *www.foodcoop.com/*

In the future, grocery shopping may be a simple matter of dialing up an online service or using a personal barcode scanner to order groceries from your home. Several experts note that Peapod Grocery and Delivery Service – an online shopping system in use by Safeway in San Francisco and by Jewel in Chicago – is already up and running. In fact, shop-by-modem services are sprouting up like mushrooms. Kroger in Ohio now offers its inventory via the World Wide Web, and the Smart-Food Co-Op of Cambridge, MA – which lays claims to the distinction of being "The First Supermarket on the Internet!" – has a six-figure tally for the number of folks who have "visited" the co-op without ever going there.

Telegrocery shopping, suggests John D. Benjamin, who is confident the service will attract customers, "is perfect for time-squeezed, two-income families." Stuart Spiegel adds that the convenience home delivery provides will spur its growth. Once that 20 percent mark is reached, Eric K. Clemons says, "online grocery shopping becomes a real alternative to the supermarket in the suburbs, not just a cost-insensitive yuppie phenomenon."

Still, some market-research bulletins, such as *The Forrester Report on People and Technology*, suggest that 20 percent represents a cap – that no more than one shopper in five will ever go online for their daily or weekly food purchases.

1997
1998
1999
2000 JOHN D. BENJAMIN, PROFESSOR, DEPARTMENT OF FINANCE AND REAL ESTATE, KOGOD COLLEGE OF BUSINESS ADMINISTRATION, THE AMERICAN UNIVERSITY
2001
2002
2003
2004
2005 ERIC K. CLEMONS, PROFESSOR OF OPERATIONS AND INFORMATION MANAGEMENT, THE WHARTON SCHOOL, UNIVERSITY OF PENNSYLVANIA
2005 STEVEN J. JOHNSON, MANAGING PARTNER FOR CONSUMER PRODUCTS, ANDERSEN CONSULTING
2005 FRED SCHNEIDER, EXECUTIVE DIRECTOR OF SMART STORE, ANDERSEN CONSULTING'S R & D CENTER FOR THE FOOD AND PACKAGED GOODS INDUSTRY
2006
2007
2008
2009
2010
2011
2012
2013
2014
2015 RICHARD FERNANDES, EXECUTIVE VICE PRESIDENT OF INTERACTIVE SERVICES, CUC INTERNATIONAL
2015 STUART SPIEGEL, VICE PRESIDENT AND GENERAL MANAGER OF INTERACTIVE SHOPPING AT QVC
2016
2017
2018
2019
2020

VR SUNGLASSES

2009

Rarely has a technology caught on as quickly or suffered from its hype as "virtual reality" has. Based on media coverage of forward-thinkers like Jaron Lanier, for example, many expected a 3-D drug trip, an out-of-body experience, or a new identity, only to try a VR system and find themselves in a slow videogame.

VR describes a computer-generated environment users access and experience through interfaces such as specially equipped gloves, goggles, and helmets. Once hooked up to the electronic interfaces, the user has the impression of being inside an artificial environment, of moving within it and reacting to it spatially, as if one were, say, moving about a room. Experiencing VR is much more than operating a joystick and then seeing some change in an image on a screen before you; in VR, the "screen" extends in every direction, and each movement you make is reproduced within the virtual environment.

In science fiction novelist William Gibson's *Virtual Light*, this technology no longer requires the cumbersome helmets it does today, but instead can be achieved merely by putting on a very special pair of sunglasses. When we asked our experts when and if we could expect such an advance, few were optimistic – unless we downgraded our expectations to glasses that functioned less like virtual reality and more like computer monitors, enabling the wearer to read emails or peruse spreadsheets or word files. In this downscaled version, the inside lens of the sunglasses serves as a computer screen and cannot provide immersive, 3-D animation. For the foreseeable future, "VR" specs come into focus only as monitors.

URLS/FURTHER READING
Atlantis Cyberspace – 3D Max. vr-atlantis.com/home_vr/consumer_vr/html/cm3.htm **Atlantis Cyberspace – Virtual I-glasses.** vr-atlantis.com/home_vr/consumer_vr /html/cm2.htm **Virtual I-O.** www.vio.com/ **What People are Doing with VR.** 141.142.3-134/Cyberia/VETopLevels/VR.Overview.contz.html

DENISE CARUSO, DIGITAL COMMERCE COLUMNIST FOR *THE NEW YORK TIMES*, EXECUTIVE PRODUCER OF THE SPOTLIGHT CONFERENCE ON INTERACTIVE MEDIA

ROBERT JACOBSON, FOUNDER AND PRESIDENT, WORLDESIGN INC.

DON NORMAN, VICE PRESIDENT, ADVANCED TECHNOLOGY, APPLE COMPUTER/2010 (FOR NICHE MARKETS)

JOHN MARKOFF, REPORTER, *THE NEW YORK TIMES*, AUTHOR OF *CYBERPUNK: OUTLAWS AND HACKERS ON THE COMPUTER FRONTIER*

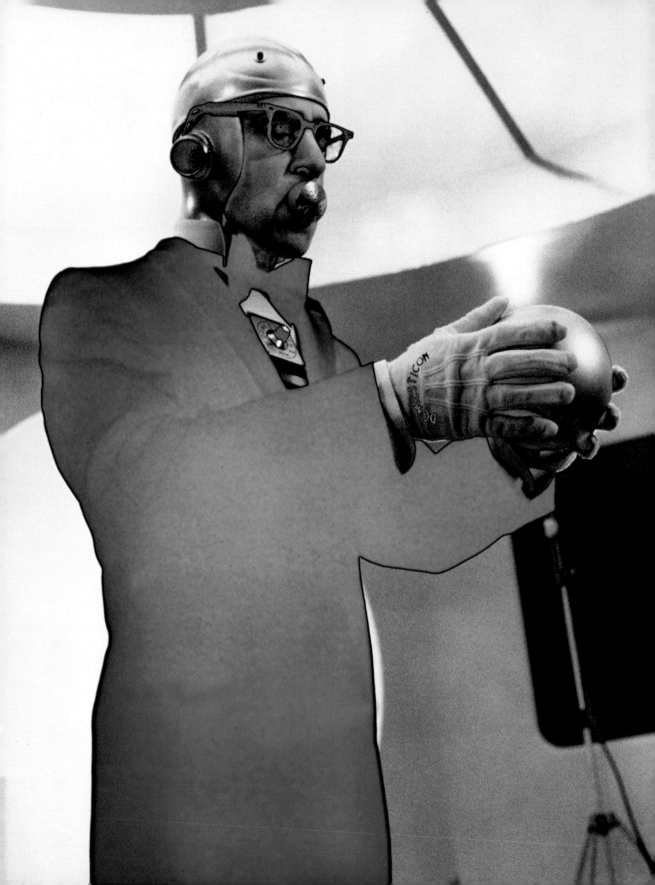

ORGASMATRON

Woody Allen's movie *Sleeper* turned many on to the idea of a brain-stimulating device that could deliver an orgasm on demand, and any number of variations have titillated the imagination since the film's 1973 release. Talk about safe sex: imagine owning a headset you could pull on like a ski cap and use to deliver a stress-reducing orgasm without any interpersonal hassle. Not only would it be convenient, it could dramatically improve the prospects for world peace.

More than 20 years after *Sleeper,* the closest things to orgasmatrons remain vibrators, which stimulate one's genitals (or other erogenous zones) and induce an orgasm the old-fashioned, manual way. Of course, vibrators have come a long way, and a few, including the Sybian, already qualify in Isadora Alman's book as orgasmatrons. (A visit to a local shop that rents the Sybian proved it a mighty saddle of pleasure.)

Richard Kadrey predicts that before there's a neuroelectric orgasmatron, there will be neurochemical one, an orgasm-in-a-pill. Nancie S. Martin, meanwhile, thinks an orgasmatron puts way too much emphasis on orgasms as a goal, instead of as a part of a total sexual experience. Howard Rheingold thinks the device already exists, but that "the inventor has not been able to leave home to get to the patent office."

URLS/FURTHER READING
Antique Vibrator Museum. *www.goodvibes.com/museum.html* Cyber-Sex-Toys. *www.sextoy.com/sextoy.html*
Sybian. *www.romantasy.com/cyboutique/sybian/*

ISADORA ALMAN, "ASK ISADORA" SYNDICATED COLUMNIST AND SEX AND RELATIONSHIP COUNSELOR

HOWARD RHEINGOLD, AUTHOR OF *VIRTUAL COMMUNITY, VIRTUAL REALITY,* AND EDITOR OF *THE MILLENNIUM WHOLE EARTH CATALOG*

RICHARD KADREY, EDITOR OF *COVERT CULTURE SOURCEBOOK* AND AUTHOR OF *KAMIKAZE L'AMOUR*

NANCIE S. MARTIN, PRESIDENT OF JOUISANCE PRODUCTIONS AND FORMER EDITOR OF *PLAYGIRL*

SMART DRUGS
2010

URLS/FURTHER READING
The Cognitive Enhancement Research Institute's Smart Drug News. *www.ceri.com* Smart Drug/Nootropic Info. *www.damicon.fi/sd/* Nutrition Square – Better Thinking
Through Chemistry. *www.uta.fi/~samu/SMARTS2.html* Advanced Research 2000. *206.155.34.8:80/ar2000/Welcome.html*

JOHN MORGAN, M.D., PROFESSOR OF PHARMACOLOGY, CITY UNIVERSITY OF NEW YORK MEDICAL SCHOOL, AND MEMBER OF THE ADVISORY BOARD OF THE DRUG POLICY FOUNDATION

ALEXANDER SHULGIN, M.D., CHEMIST/PHARMACOLOGIST, UNIVERSITY OF CALIFORNIA, BERKELEY; AND CO-AUTHOR OF *PIHKAL: A CHEMICAL LOVE STORY*

TIMOTHY LEARY, PH.D, PHILOSOPHER

MICHAEL ALDRICH, PH.D., CURATOR, FITZ HUGH LUDLOW MEMORIAL LIBRARY

ANDREW WEIL, M.D., AUTHOR OF *SPONTANEOUS HEALING AND NATURAL HEALTH, NATURAL MEDICINE*

If "smart drinks" raised and then dashed expectations for brain nutrients at nightclubs in the late 1980s and early 1990s, some nutritional supplements currently on the market – often referred to as nootropics – can serve as vitamins for one's grey matter. Indeed, nootropic purveyors claim these agents can slow the onset of senility, aid in repair of brain damage, and stimulate brain activity in a manner generally associated with caffeine.

Smart drugs definitely have their true believers, such as Durk Pearson and Sandy Shaw, who have been promoting them since the 1970s, and Ward Dean, a co-author of a series from Health Freedom Publications called *Smart Drugs & Nutrients: How to Improve Your Memory and Increase Your Intelligence Using the Latest Discoveries in Neuroscience.* Certain drugs, including Piracetam and Deprenyl, prescribed by physicians to treat Parkinson's disease and memory disturbances, could be considered smart drugs as well.

Still, debate continues about their efficacy for the average, active person. While most of the experts we surveyed agreed that eventually drugs or nutrients will come along and settle the debate once and for all, they note that their widespread availability in the United States will be delayed by Food and Drug Adminstration protocols – and that by the time they are available, what people consider "smart" will have changed, too. Thus even though Dr. John Morgan speculates that amphetamines may increase IQ scores, all of our experts agreed that the IQ test is an outmoded gauge of intelligence. Examples like these lead Dr. Alexander Shulgin to conclude that the "limitation is not developing a smart drug; it's learning how to measure its effectiveness."

ROBOT SURGEON (IN A PILL)

2010

URLS/FURTHER READING
Why Micro Robots?: isx.com/~isr/WhyMR.html Medical Applications of Robots. robby.caltech.edu/~jwb/medical.html Autonomous Human-Body Traversing
Micro-Robots: Technological Challenges and Future Potential. ralph.biomed.mcgill.ca/EMBC95/symposia/hunter.html#3

Maybe too many lipids are clogging your coronary arteries, or a growing tumor threatens to pinch a nerve, or you're bleeding internally because of an ulcer or a traffic accident. Instead of going under the knife, imagine that you could ingest a robot that while traveling throughout your body on a preprogrammed course could perform internal surgery, clear away life-threatening fat deposits, dispatch tumors, or cinch up wounds.

Even if not all of these scenarios are foreseeable, the surgeons we consulted expect robot surgeons you can swallow to be a reality as soon as 2010. Still, the inner-space "fantastic voyagers" predicted for 2010 will not yet be small enough to cleanse the bloodstream. Instead, early model robot surgeons might be suppositories that don't melt or horse pills that target trouble in your digestive tract.

Obstacles to such ingestable robots are formidable. As Dr. Richard Satava points out, scientists will have to create a miniscule and remarkably flexible and mobile robot that can maneuver around with ease inside "such difficult terrain as the colon or a blood vessel." Moreover, many trials will have to be initiated and successfully completed before physicians will feel comfortable sending microdevices inside us to snip our polyps. For robots that negotiate the bloodstream like T cells, nanotechnology (see page 39) holds some promise, but even though it's not physically impossible, nanotechnology still requires such extreme technical advances that few are willing to circle its arrival date on a calendar.

(see page 39)

DAVID VINING, M.D., ASSISTANT PROFESSOR OF ABDOMINAL IMAGING, BOWMAN GRAY SCHOOL OF MEDICINE, WAKE FOREST UNIVERSITY

ANTHONY DIGIOIA III, M.D., CO-DIRECTOR, CENTER FOR MEDICAL ROBOTICS AND COMPUTER-ASSISTED SURGERY, CARNEGIE MELLON UNIVERSITY

PHILIP GREEN, M.D., PRESIDENT, TELESURGICAL CORPORATION

RICHARD SATAVA, M.D., PROGRAM MANAGER, ADVANCED BIOMEDICAL TECHNOLOGY, ADVANCED RESEARCH PROJECTS AGENCY

2000 2001 2002 2003 2004 2005 2006 2007 2008 2009 **2010** 2010 2010 2010 2011 2012 2013 2014 2015 2016 2017 2018 2019 2020 2021 2022 2023

THE AUDIO CD BECOMES A FORMAT OF SECOND CHOICE

2010

Audio CDs – those shiny disks that displaced vinyl LPs and cassettes as the primary vehicle for recorded tunes – will soon face their turn as technological lame ducks, or so say enough pundits to unnerve some music aficionados.

On the face of it, such a development doesn't seem to follow the trend in the music industry. Save a few musicians and audio engineers who prefer the "warmth" of analog sound, recording studios have gone exclusively digital, and the day when we'll be able to record on blank CDs at home is also drawing near (see "Affordable Home CD Recorders," page 3).

And yet, CDs are only one of the ways digitized music can be stored and delivered. "I truly believe the life and death of CDs is not an issue of technology," says Ron Gompertz. "It's more a practical issue, an issue of re-fixturing.... How long the CD lasts will have more to do with habits than with technology."

The reason this is so, Gompertz notes, is that the technology that could replace CDs has already arrived. As Peter Gotcher points out, Net-savvy music lovers already sample and buy new compositions via Internet-linked computers. As bandwidth and computer memory become less limiting factors, Gotcher and others say, it's a safe bet a significant number of listeners will use their computers as listening kiosks and mail-order catalogs. Listeners will purchase and download audio files, some in real time, and will refer to Web sites for artwork, articles, and "digital liner notes."

Techno-audiophiles, meanwhile, predict that just about the time CDs become as versatile as cassettes, a new format will enter the marketplace. At first, Ivan Berger suggests, it may be a variation on the CD, like the prototypic DVD (digital video disk, or disc, depending on your source), which will double as a CD-ROM and an audio CD. Or, opines Gompertz, the new format might be a flash card or a modification of the digital audio tape, DAT – only this time retailers will regard them as essential to their business.

Compact Disc, How Good Is It?: A compact history and thoughtful consideration of the prospects for CD technology by David Schofield. ppewww.ph.gla.ac.uk/~gowdy /Amiga/AmigaReport/AR207_Sections/P1-11.HTML CD-E: The Future of Compact Disc Technology: CD-E stands for compact disc erasable and this site introduces the technology these folks say will complement CD-R (recordable). www.4cdr.com/info/misc_info/cd_erasable.htm Philips Compact Disc Interactive: The makers of multimedia CDs on why they think theirs rule. www-eu.philips.com/sv/newtech/cdi.html Recordable CD: The Laser Printer of the Digital World: An info rich, if slightly evangelical essay on the CD-R. www.sigcat.org/vgn2.htm

IVAN BERGER, TECHNICAL EDITOR, *AUDIO MAGAZINE*

PETER GOTCHER, PRESIDENT AND CEO, DIGIDESIGN, INC.

RON GOMPERTZ, PRESIDENT, HEYDAY RECORDS, CO-CREATOR OF *CYBORGASM*

JERRY HARRISON, AUDIO PRODUCER AND FORMER TALKING HEAD

ROGER DRESSLER, TECHNICAL DIRECTOR, DOLBY LABORATORIES

BOTTOM LINE: LOOK FOR THE AUDIO CD TO BE A FORMAT OF SECOND CHOICE

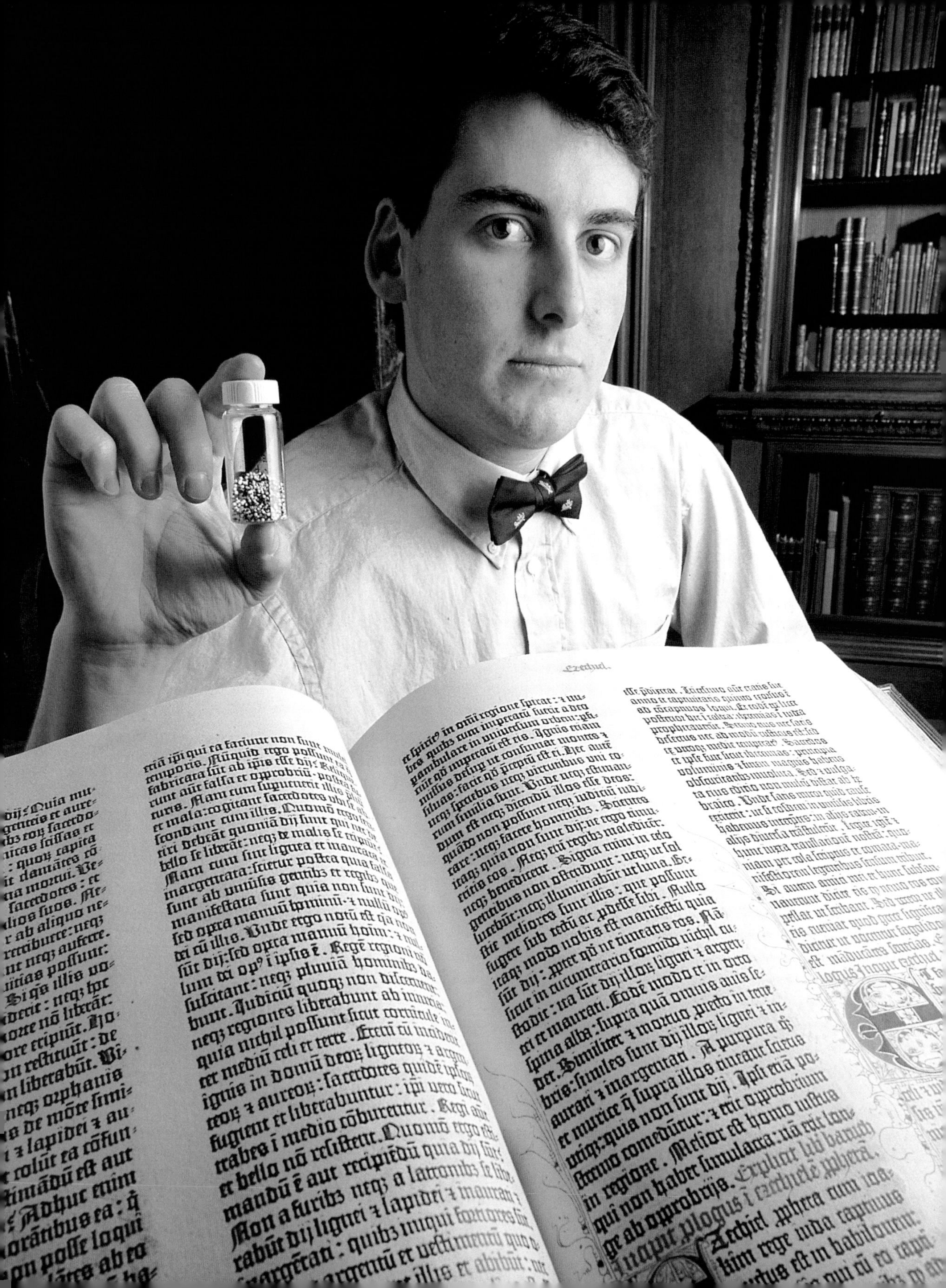

THE BOOK GOES DIGITAL

2013

The book is not dead yet. A laptop isn't half so portable or versatile as a paperback, and few are those who want (or have the option) to do all their reading on screen. And it's funny how the most pessimistic news yet about the future of the book arrives at a time when more books are hot off presses than ever before. What's more, the publisher of this book banks on the contention that books remain an unparalleled medium for certain kinds of thought and human expression. Nevertheless, lab tinkerers are currently creating scenarios to present the text you are reading right now in ways that could save forests and could well prove preferable for most of what is now published on paper – just as CD-ROMs have become a medium of first choice for encyclopedias, and the World Wide Web a viable alternative to an in-box full of trade journals and newsletters.

One such scenario involves Joe Jacobson's electronic pages, currently in development at the MIT Media Lab, which are digital displays that read like printed pages, except that they can be erased and reused any number of times. Jacobson's digital pages recast the book as a vibrant electronic Etch-a-Sketch.

Of course, the mere feasibility of such scenarios won't seal the book's fate. For one thing, not even the cleverest invention will be welcomed by publishers and booksellers if it means costly changes in book production methods, distribution patterns, and in-store displays. Furthermore, if books go digital and get distributed over the Net, Net-linked computers will have to continue to proliferate (especially in homes), and be free in libraries, before a majority of readers will peruse PCs as often as they browse bookshelves. Finally, the fact that a book is a fetish as well as an information medium cannot be ignored. When asked what advantages a computer could offer to make reading on screen preferable to the printed page, critic Sven Birkerts replied, "There are no attributes that I can imagine that would make screen reading preferable to page reading – just as there is no prosthesis I can think of that could improve love-making."

These factors aside, one glaring fact remains: digital forms of books cost as little as one-tenth of their paper counterparts. Comparing notes with current editors of venerable literary magazines (such as Wen Stephenson) or with "computer-resistant" booksellers (such as Leona Weiss) reveals the same conviction: that, in Weiss's words, "all nonfiction books, reference works, journals, and such will be available to read on screen or to download to one's computer within 15 years."

MIT Media Lab Projects 1995: Place to begin for information on Dr. Joseph Jacobson's electronic Paper Books. www.media.mit.edu/groups/tw/jacobson........... The "leading bookstore on the Web." http://www.amazon.com Project Gutenberg: Outline of goals and how it's sustained. www.uwa.ac.nz/non-local/gutenberg/ The New Publishing: Technology's Impact on the Publishing Industry Over the Next Decade: An extensive report. anima.wis.net/ATLAS/Electronic_Literature/TheNewPublish ing.html Internet Roundtable Society's Interview with Sven Birkerts: More from Birkerts about why the Digital Revolution ain't got no soul. www.rsociety.com /recent/tranbirk.html Find Bind Electronic Books. www.axxis.com/~mfine/fbooks.html

MIKE SHATZKIN, PRESIDENT, THE IDEA LOGICAL COMPANY, INC., AND CONSULTANT TO PUBLISHERS ON NEW TECHNOLOGIES

SVEN BIRKERTS, AUTHOR OF THE GUTENBERG ELEGIES: THE FATE OF READING IN AN ELECTRONIC AGE

LEONA WEISS, CO-OWNER AND BUYER FOR A CLEAN WELL-LIGHTED PLACE FOR BOOKS, SAN FRANCISCO, CA

WEN STEPHENSON, EDITOR, NEW MEDIA, THE ATLANTIC MONTHLY

JASON EPSTINE, EDITOR, RANDOM HOUSE

Suppose flying to London took only three hours (as opposed to seven), Tokyo only four-and-a-half (rather than 10), or Cape Town only 12 (instead of 23). Few of us wouldn't jump at the chance for high-speed air travel, but opportunities for supersonic flight have always depended on the size of one's bank account. After all, even though Concorde has been making trans-Atlantic flights for 16 years, a flight from New York to London still costs US$4,000 – almost 10 times the subsonic price. This price gap, our experts say, will shrink early in the next century and may eventually disappear.

While it's true that aerospace technology hasn't had a milestone to match Sir Frank Whittle's jet engine, patented 65 years ago, our experts report promising advances, including technology that will enable second-generation supersonic jets to fly at Mach 2.4 (1,600 miles per hour) while being environmentally friendlier.

Boeing and others have justified the development of high-speed civil transport (HSCT) planes in studies suggesting that by 2005 worldwide air traffic will double, and better than double between North America and Asia. Consistent with these studies, several experts we polled predict that rapid growth in trans-Pacific air travel will help make HSCT economically viable. Along with higher speeds and lower costs, they say, new supersonic planes will carry 300 passengers and some cargo (as opposed to the Concorde's 100 passengers and no cargo).

High-Speed Civil Transport Homepage: Place to learn more about the US Mach 2.4, the successor to the Concorde. members.aol.com/HSCT/ High Speed Civil Transport – Vital Investment in America's Future: Homepage for those making the political push to bring supersonic travel to the mass market. www.lerc.nasa.gov/Othe Groups/HSR/hsct.html Air France Concorde: Homepage of the Mach 2 and Air France. www.airfrance.fr/prod/ccr/default.html The High Speed Civil Transport: M the Mach 2.4 with plenty of stats. heart.engr.csulb.edu/ae/hsct.html

McDONNELL DOUGLAS CORPORATION

JERRY GREY, PH.D., DIRECTOR OF AEROSPACE AND SCIENCE POLICY, AMERICAN INSTITUTE OF AERONAUTICS AND ASTRONAUTICS

LOUIS J. WILLIAMS, DIRECTOR OF HIGH-SPEED RESEARCH DIVISION, NASA

MIKE DERCHIN, AIRLINE AND AEROSPACE ANALYST, TIGER MANAGEMENT

KELLY SCOTT, TRANSPORTATION ANALYST, OFFICE OF TECHNOLOGY ASSESSMENT, U.S. CONGRESS

ONLINE ADVERTISING ECLIPSES TV COMMERCIALS

2014

Whether you consider advertising pop art or a waste of time and space, it is the fuel that drives a medium to the masses, and its role in media sponsorship will continue in a world gone digital. Even so, the experts we surveyed disagree on how advertisers will divide their expenditures among the various media, and they wonder aloud whether the Internet will ever displace television as a vehicle for commercials.

According to Forrester Research Inc., ad agencies spent more than US$37 million on their clients' behalf during 1995. Meanwhile, McCann-Erickson, the worldwide ad agency, reports that agencies shelled out US$12 *billion* for television spots, evidence that digital ads have many, many screens to cover before they eclipse their "cool" media cousins. (*Cool*, by the way, was a term used by Marshall McLuhan for media that provide less complete data and require more of the viewer. A photograph, to McLuhan's eye, was "hot," a cartoon, "cool." By extension, an info-laden Web site is "hot," a 30-second iconic TV spot, "cool.")

Several believe online ad expenditures will overtake costs of tele-vision commercials only if TV and computers merge. If they do, Cathy Taylor predicts that TV and Internet broadcasters will absorb both budgets.

Still, Kathy Biro forecasts that if and when our TVs go online (see "An Interactive TV in Every Home," page 143), the lion's share of consumers will still prefer perusing the passive media, and advertisers will follow their lead. Says Biro, "Compared to channel surfing from your couch, the computer will always feel like too much work."

Netways Marketing Group: homepage of a marketing group that's trying to develop superior new media. www.netways.com/netways/background.html Forrester Research: Homepage of one of the leading monitors of the new media business. www.forrester.com/ The New York Festivals: Updated each month, this site tracks more than 14,000 new examples each year of print, radio, television, and interactive ads. www.nyfests.com/index.html Advertising Research Foundation: Homepage of a consortium devoted to improving the quality of advertising. www.amic.com/arf/ Nielsen Interactive Services: The company that has a virtual monopoly monitoring TV traffic tries to flex its muscles online. www.nielsenmedia.com/

CATHY TAYLOR, SENIOR EDITOR OF NEW MEDIA, ADWEEK MAGAZINE

G. M. O'CONNELL, FOUNDING PARTNER, MODEM MEDIA

ANDY SPADE, CREATIVE DIRECTOR, TBWA CHIAT/DAY

KATHY BIRO, PRESIDENT, STRATEGIC INTERACTIVE GROUP (A BRONNER SLOSBERG HUMPHREY COMPANY)

RICHARD KIRSCHENBAUM, CO-CHAIR, KIRSCHENBAUM, BOND & PARTNERS

2000
2002
2004
2006
2007
2008
2010
2012
2014
2016
2018
2020
2022
2024
2025
2026
2028
2030
2032
2034
2036
2038
2040
2042
2044
UNLIKELY
UNLIKELY

If you purchased salmon, trout, catfish, or shrimp at the supermarket recently, the chances are better than even that you bought and ate seafood that wasn't harvested from the open ocean, but instead was raised on a fish farm through aquaculture. These and many other varieties of seafood are cultivated in undersea "barnyards," in enclosed coastal areas, and even in land-based tanks. According to Dr. Rebecca Goldburg of the Environmental Defense Fund, aquaculture already accounts for 19 percent of fish harvests worldwide and is a US$87 million industry in South Australia.

Asked if aquaculture would someday supply most of the seafood consumed in the United States, our panel of food and nutrition experts said it would certainly come to pass, but cited as limiting factors the adverse effects overzealous aquaculture could have on the marine habitats they utilize. Among the potential drawbacks were pollution – from fish feces (ammonia), uneaten fish food, and hazardous chemicals and antibiotics used to control diseases during production – and alteration of aquatic ecosystems, from the removal of mangrove forest to competition with wild fish populations by escapees.

Still, while these imperfections were apparent, the incentives for increased fish farming were also clear. Ellen Martin says unequivocally that "the exhaustion of wild fish populations will dictate that ownership is the only way to control the supply of seafood." Mahmoud El-Begearmi speculates that FDA regulations instituted to protect consumers from harmful bacteria in seafood may also quicken the growth of aquaculture.

/EDF-Letter/1996/Jan/l_aquacult.html Hydro/Aquatic Technologies: So You Want to Be a Fish Farmer!: Advice for the would-be fish harvester. www.intercom.net/biz /aquaedu/hatech/pages/runaquac.html Aquaculture – Industry at a Glance: Excellent overview of aquaculture by one of the industry's leading agencies, Primary Industries of South Australia. dmo.slsa.gov.au/sagov/agencies/pisa/sa_i_gl/aqu.htm Agriculture, Fisheries and Food (Province of British Columbia): A serviceable introduction to aquaculture in Q & A format with an emphasis on British Columbia. bbs.qp.gov.bc.ca/bcmaff/cprofile/aquafish.htm

MAHMOUD EL-BEGEARMI, PH.D., NUTRITION AND FOOD SAFETY SPECIALIST, UNIVERSITY OF MAINE COOPERATIVE EXTENSION

ELLEN MARTIN, SCIENCE COMMUNICATIONS, DNA PLANT TECHNOLOGY

MANFRED KROGER, PH.D., PROFESSOR OF FOOD SCIENCE, PENNSYLVANIA STATE UNIVERSITY

JIM McCAMANT, EDITOR, AGBIOTECH STOCK LETTER

1994 1996 1998 2000 2000 2002 2004 2006 2008 2010 2012 **2014** 2016 2018 2020 2022 2024 2025 2026 2028 2030 2032 2034 2036 2038 2040 2042

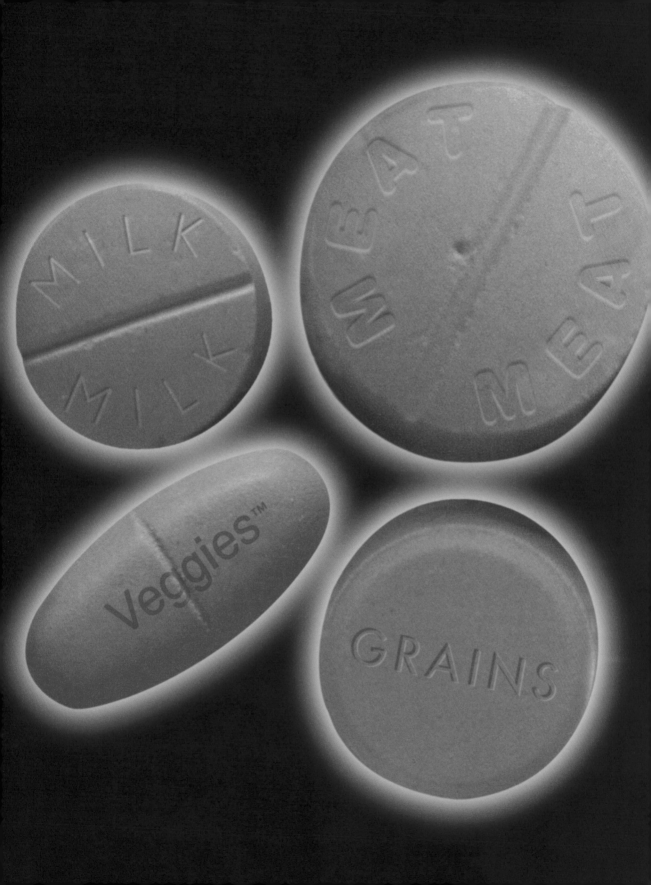

FOOD TABLETS PROVIDE COMPLETE NUTRITION

2015

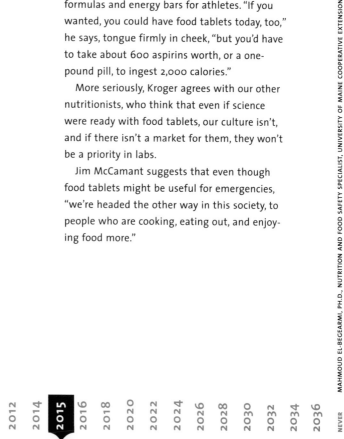

You couldn't ask for faster food than a meal's or even a day's worth of nutrition all from a pill the size of an aspirin – and convenience is but a secondary reason, behind ending famine world-wide, that the food tablet remains a compelling fantasy. As Manfred Kroger points out, we have similar products now, citing as examples baby formulas and energy bars for athletes. "If you wanted, you could have food tablets today, too," he says, tongue firmly in cheek, "but you'd have to take about 600 aspirins worth, or a one-pound pill, to ingest 2,000 calories."

More seriously, Kroger agrees with our other nutritionists, who think that even if science were ready with food tablets, our culture isn't, and if there isn't a market for them, they won't be a priority in labs.

Jim McCamant suggests that even though food tablets might be useful for emergencies, "we're headed the other way in this society, to people who are cooking, eating out, and enjoy-ing food more."

www.gerber.com/index.html The Feeding Gastronomy Homepage: The site for those who get their nutrition through a tube and want to go gourmet. www.iinet.com.au/%7Escarffam/gtube.html Nutren: Homepage to the makers of Nutren, "setting the standard in tube feeding." www.txdirect.net/corp/tdr /enterals.htm Food for Space Flight: Driving the invention of liquid and tablet foods are those in flight. What the Apollo astronauts ate and more. www.msfc.nasa.gov/mol/crew/food.html

MANFRED KROGER, PH.D., PROFESSOR OF FOOD SCIENCE, PENNSYLVANIA STATE UNIVERSITY

JIM McCAMANT, EDITOR, AGBIOTECH STOCK LETTER

MAHMOUD EL-BEGEARMI, PH.D., NUTRITION AND FOOD SAFETY SPECIALIST, UNIVERSITY OF MAINE COOPERATIVE EXTENSION

ELLEN MARTIN, SCIENCE COMMUNICATIONS, DNA PLANT TECHNOLOGY

1990 1992 1994 1996 1998 2000 2002 2004 2006 2008 2010 2012 2014 **2015** 2016 2018 2020 2022 2024 2026 2028 2030 2032 2034 2036 NEVER NEVER

HOLOPHONE

2016

Imagine a phone that displays a 3-D image so realistic it's as if the person you called is sitting right across from you. According to the experts in holography we consulted, this scenario – given a boost in the popular imagination by Princess Leia's SOS in *Star Wars* – is not so much a matter of developing the technology to project the hologram (that's already here) as a matter of connecting people with the bandwidth required to transmit real-time 3-D images. In fact, the prospects for holography make the hoopla surrounding virtual reality seem misplaced.

It will take time, of course, before the required bandwidth will be available and/or installed in a majority of homes (see "Fiber to the Home," page 65), but Mark Diamond thinks that once that hurdle has been over-

come, "intelligent" optical materials will operate on both ends of the fiber-optic line. Such materials will efficiently and naturally compress holographic images, he says, eliminating the need for powerful computers to reproduce the holograms on either end.

Stephen A. Benton points out that two years ago, the MIT Media Lab sent a hologram through 70 meters of coaxial cable, but he believes the first holographic phones are likely to employ improved "lenticular imaging," the quasi-holographic technology used on 3-D postcards.

More philosophically, Diamond reflects that once holograms have become a regular part of our lives (and their visual quality is convincing), they will change the way we look at the world. "We will see a return to the ancient belief that information is dispersed everywhere, within us and without, and we'll adjust to the perception that things are weightless," Diamond says. "[Holography] will give us new metaphors to live by."

Coherent Laser Vision System: Profile of a technology that could enable holophones. www.glnet.org/on/mt/mt/technol/mtcrvssaln.htm A Novel Crystalline Material for Recording Holographic Moving Images: Biased, but useful introduction to a new way to record holographic images. www.info.hqs.cae.ntt.jp/RD/1994rev/basic /baco2.html Holophile Inc. – Spectral Imagery: Homepage for a device that lets you convey a message as Princess Leia did in Star Wars. www.comix.com/~barefoot /people.htm Diffraction-Specific Fringe Computation for Electro-Holography: Doctoral dissertation on technology necessary for transmission of holograms, by Mark Lucente. lucente.www.media.mit.edu/people/lucente/holo/PhDthesis/contents_psz.html

STEPHEN A. BENTON, PH.D., ALLEN PROFESSOR OF MEDIA ARTS AND SCIENCES, SPATIAL IMAGING GROUP, MEDIA LAB, MASSACHUSETTS INSTITUTE OF TECHNOLOGY

TUNG HON JEONG, PROFESSOR OF PHYSICS, AND DIRECTOR OF THE CENTER OF PHOTONICS STUDIES, LAKE FOREST COLLEGE

MARK DIAMOND, FOUNDER, DIAMOND IMAGES, INC., AND CREATIVE DIRECTOR AND VICE PRESIDENT, 3-D WORLDWIDE HOLOGRAMS, INC.

JAMES FISCHBACH, PRESIDENT AND CEO, AMERICAN PROPYLAEA, A COMMERCIAL HOLOGRAPHY DEVELOPER

EMMETT LEITH, PH.D., PROFESSOR OF ELECTRICAL ENGINEERING AND COMPUTER SCIENCE, UNIVERSITY OF MICHIGAN

1994 1996 1998 2000 2002 2004 2005 2006 2008 2010 2012 2014 2015 **2016** 2018 2020 2022 2024 2026 2028 2030 2032 2034 2036 2038 2040 2050

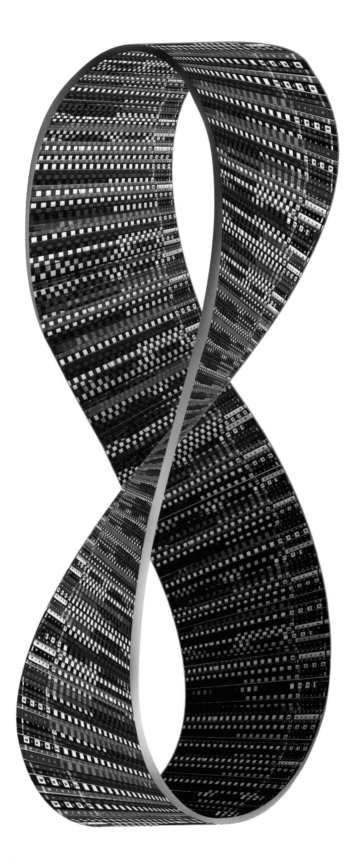

FIRST LARGE, PUBLIC VIRTUAL LIBRARY

2016

Fortunately, public libraries won't be closing their doors anytime soon, nor will software applications put skilled reference librarians out on the street. Still, computer databases have replaced bulky card catalogs, new media have broadened the range of library materials available for browsing, and networked computers have given rise to the concept of a library without walls – a wealth of virtual shelves full of virtual books, each containing texts to be read on screen or downloaded rather than "checked out."

Even as Project Gutenberg is making thousands of texts in the public domain available electronically – its stated goal is to bring 10,000 electronic texts of classic literature, reference materials, and tie-ins to popular movies, TV, and radio programming online by 2001 – our experts predict that most libraries will offer complementary electronic and print collections. (Online bookseller Amazon.com, meanwhile, aspires to have every book in print on sale at their Web site in the next decade – roughly one million titles.) The first large libraries to go strictly virtual, they say, will be at universities or other specialized facilities that serve a geographically scattered community of users.

"A good candidate for the first virtual library would be a multinational corporation's library that people use around the clock," Clifford Lynch says. For a public library to make the conversion, Ellen Poisson notes, would require the people it serves to have universal online access.

But Ken Dowlin questions whether a virtual library can really be a library. A collection of books, he contends, does not necessarily constitute a library, because libraries are also "socialization facilities, communications facilities, protected public spaces – even icons of the community."

Aether Madness/Gutenberg Project: The Gutenberg Project introduced by the authors of *Aether Madness*. *www.aether.com/aether/gutenberg.html* The Future of Electronic Text: The virtues of e-text for libraries and researchers by Richard J. Pugh. *www.ids.net/~rjpugh/future.html* Future InfoSystems Virtual Digital Library: An early online library with search capabilities. Tell them what you think. *futureinfo.com/fis/digitallibrary.html* Stanford Digital Libraries Project: Report on an effort to build a user-friendly, "universal" online library. *diglib.stanford.edu/diglib/* NSF Announces Awards for Digital Libraries Research. *http:cs.berkeley.edu:80/~wilensky /proj-html/nsf-press-release.html*

CLIFFORD LYNCH, DIRECTOR OF LIBRARY AUTOMATION, UNIVERSITY OF CALIFORNIA

KEN DOWLIN, CITY LIBRARIAN OF SAN FRANCISCO, AND AUTHOR OF *THE ELECTRONIC LIBRARY: THE PROMISE AND THE PROCESS*

BOB ZICH, DIRECTOR OF ELECTRONIC PROGRAMS, LIBRARY OF CONGRESS

ELLEN POISSON, ASSISTANT DIRECTOR FOR ELECTRONIC RESOURCES AT THE NEW YORK PUBLIC LIBRARY'S SCIENCE, INDUSTRY AND BUSINESS LIBRARY

HECTOR GARCIA-MOLINA, PRINCIPAL INVESTIGATOR FOR THE STANFORD DIGITAL LIBRARY PROJECT, STANFORD UNIVERSITY

2000 2002 2004 2005 2006 2008 2010 2012 2014 **2016** 2018 2020 2022 2024 2026 2028 2030 2032 2034 2036 2038 2040 2042 2044 2048 2050 UNLIKELY

AUTOMATED HIGHWAY SYSTEMS IN U.S. CITIES

2017

On-board computers continue to make cars smarter than ever. For example, 1996 Lincoln Continentals have a factory-installed option known as RESCU, essentially an emergency car phone. Activated by a push button on an overhead console, it puts an emergency dispatcher on a "speaker phone," enabling a trapped or injured motorist to call for help. Solar units (see "Solar-Powered Automobiles," page 21), meanwhile, offer new sources of auxiliary power for cars and will likely help to recharge the batteries of electric cars when these vehicles are no longer the novelty they once were (see "More Than 50 Percent Drive Electric Cars," page 121).

Each "smart car" innovation has rekindled the dream of placing a car on autopilot and zipping home along a route preprogrammed to avoid gridlock, and three of the experts we consulted assured us this notion will not remain a dream indefinitely. Thomas B. Deen, Richard L. Klimisch, and Noah Rifkin cite the Intermodal Surface Transportation Efficiency Act of 1991, which aims for testing of an automated highway system by 1997. (In fact, Congress has allocated billions of dollars for the development and evaluation of highway systems for U.S. cities.) The others we consulted also predict

that a full-fledged highway-automation experiment will be conducted around the turn of the century, and that deployment will follow.

Despite the promise of trials, our experts caution against expectations that automated highway systems will become standard in the next couple of decades. For one thing, implementing the required infrastructure changes will be a massive undertaking; for another, motorists will also have to add to their vehicles a device (something akin to a cruise control system) that allows a highway system to assume control of the car. Rupert Welch, for one, thinks that this technology will jack up car prices by thousands of dollars, and that the combination of high cost and limited use will keep automated highway systems impractical in the short term. Finally, there's the concern that some motorists will be put off by the use of global positioning satellites (GPS), sure to be an integral component in automated highway navigation. GPS can track a vehicle – and therefore its occupants – everywhere it goes, perhaps diminishing one's sense of freedom behind the wheel and narrowing the "open road."

TASC – Opportunities for Intelligent Vehicle Highway Systems: Fairly technical discussion on developing IVHS. A proposal for further study. www.tasc.com/simweb /papers/IVHS/intro.htm The SmartPath Simulation and Animation Package: Brief on research by SmartPath Project at the University of California, Berkeley. www.path .eecs.berkeleyedu/~delnaz/SmartPath/sm.html Texas A&M IVHS Research Center of Excellence: Brochure for a major transportation research center at Texas A&M University. herman.tamu.edu/ivhsrce.html Control of Intelligent Vehicle and Highway Systems: Fairly technical introduction to a platooning architecture concept for automated traffic. robotics.eecs.berkeleyedu/~lind/ivhs.html

RUPERT WELCH, EDITOR, *INSIDE DOT AND TRANSPORTATION WEEK*

NOAH RIFKIN, DIRECTOR OF TECHNOLOGY DEPLOYMENT, UNITED STATES DEPARTMENT OF TRANSPORTATION

STEVEN E. SHLADOVER, ACTING DIRECTOR, CALIFORNIA PARTNERS FOR ADVANCED TRANSIT AND HIGHWAYS

RICHARD L. KLIMISCH, PH.D., VICE PRESIDENT OF ENGINEERING, AMERICAN AUTOMOBILE MANUFACTURERS ASSOCIATION

THOMAS B. DEEN, EXECUTIVE DIRECTOR, TRANSPORTATION RESEARCH BOARD

2000 2002 2004 2006 2008 2010 2010 2010 2012 2014 2016 **2017** 2018 2020 2022 2024 2025 2026 2028 2030 2032 2034 2036 2038 2040 2042 2044

BOYCOTT WHITE POWDER · BRING BACK HERB!

WE ARE COMING!

AUG 26

SAFE DRUGS RALLY · 11 AM
WASHINGTON SQ. PARK N.Y.C
& PEACE MARCH · 2PM

DECRIMINALIZATION OF DRUGS IN THE UNITED STATES

2019

While Steve Dnistrian, vice president of Partnership for a Drug-Free America, thinks drugs will be decriminalized only "when we decide genocide is a good idea," many drug policy activists think a "just say know" attitude is better for developing a viable harm-reduction policy. For now, those with Dnistrian's point of view set U.S. drug policy.

Changing this, our experts agree, will require initiative on the part of those opposed to the war on drugs, and, according to Dr. Alexander Shulgin, it will have to come soon. Shulgin reflects that "the speed of the erosion of our rights and freedoms is such that if decriminalization does not occur in a couple of years, it cannot occur" – until a social or political revolution takes place.

"The last couple of years," writes Shulgin, "have not led to any constructive changes in law and, although there are more and more voices speaking for the necessity of such a

change, the fact is that penalties are still being increased, urine tests more widely accepted, seizures and confiscations more commonplace and more vicious, and new drugs are still being added to the illegal lists."

Short of the overthrow of the U.S. government, the decriminalization of drugs will require that U.S. citizens first envision an alternative to the system now in place. But, our brain trust notes, arguments for the "positive enforcement" attitudes and practices now common in Spain, Holland, and Italy fall on deaf ears in the United States.

Michael Aldrich, who predicted in 1966 that marijuana would be legalized a decade later (and who notes that President Jimmy Carter almost proved him right), is now less optimistic. Aldrich views current drug policy as self-fulfilling. "Prohibition of drugs accepted by millions of users," he reflects, "is impossible without totalitarian enforcement." Ever the optimist, the late Timothy Leary expected a paradigm shift in 1996 as Americans came to their senses and called for a free-drug America.

TIMOTHY LEARY, PH.D., PHILOSOPHER

ANDREW WEIL, M.D., AUTHOR OF *SPONTANEOUS HEALING AND NATURAL HEALTH, NATURAL MEDICINE*

JOHN MORGAN, M.D., PROFESSOR OF PHARMACOLOGY, CITY UNIVERSITY OF NEW YORK, AND MEMBER OF THE ADVISORY BOARD OF THE DRUG POLICY FOUNDATION

ALEXANDER SHULGIN, M.D., CHEMIST/PHARMACOLOGIST, UNIVERSITY OF CALIFORNIA, BERKELEY, AND CO-AUTHOR OF *PIHKAL: A CHEMICAL LOVE STORY*

MICHAEL ALDRICH, PH.D., CURATOR, FITZ HUGH LUDLOW MEMORIAL LIBRARY

1990 1992 1994 1996 1998 2000 2002 2004 2006 2008 2010 2012 2014 2014 2016 2018 **2019** 2020 2022 2024 2026 2028 2030 2032 2034 2036 2050

SELF-DRIVING VEHICLES

2019

Picture hailing a cab and not having to deal with the driver's bad jokes or urban horror stories. Or imagine owning your own vehicle equipped with sensing and navigation systems such that with the flip of a switch you can turn on total cruise control and let it drive you home.

Intelligent vehicles may not yet be ready to merge with today's hectic traffic, but they exist. The system named Portable Advanced Navigation Support (PANS) developed at Carnegie Mellon University has already logged more than 6,000 "autonomous miles" aboard a Pontiac van.

If self-driving vehicles are to become available to the general public, Rodney A. Brooks believes, advances must be made in the global positioning satellites (GPS) navigation system, and some of the 4 million miles of streets, roads, and highways in the United States will have to be upgraded to accommodate autonomous vehicles. John Canny points out that "machine vision" must improve *significantly* if a robotic chauffeur is to differentiate among roadwork, graffiti, truck spills, and trees lining the streets.

Mindful of road hazards and the underrated complexity of driving, Toshio Fukuda doesn't think commuting from the suburbs to downtown in a robotic carpool will happen anytime soon. However, "self-driving taxis will be possible in limited areas of the city, where infrastructure for autonomous vehicles can be established," he says.

Still, with auto accidents responsible for 40,000 deaths and five million injuries in the United States each year, the incentive for what the U.S. Department of Transportation calls Intelligent Transportation Systems seems obvious. (See also "Automated Highway Systems in U.S. Cities," page 99.)

(See also "Automated Highway Systems in U.S. Cities," page 99.)

---

nhaa/Journal.html Intelligent Transportation Systems Testbed Vehicle: Homepage of another prototype that also redefines "cruise control." www.erim.org/TRANS /itstbv.html Telepresence Remotely Operated Vehicle: Equipment that can be controlled from a distance NASA hopes to use for reconnaissance. maas-neotek.arc.nasa .gov/TROV/trov.html NraD TeleOperated Vehicle: Features military vehicles that can be remote controlled. www.nosc.mil/robots/land/tov/tov.html VIRC: Device that could prove essential to automated cars and highways. enet.hq.ensco.com/apps/virc.html

---

Timeline:

- **2005** — JOHN CANNY, ASSOCIATE PROFESSOR OF COMPUTER SCIENCE, UNIVERSITY OF CALIFORNIA, BERKELEY
- **2010** — JOE ENGELBERGER, CHAIR, HELPMATE ROBOTICS, INC.
- **2015** — RODNEY A. BROOKS, ASSOCIATE DIRECTOR, MIT ARTIFICIAL INTELLIGENCE LABORATORY, AND CHAIR, IS ROBOTICS, INC.
- **2019** — TOSHIO FUKUDA, PROFESSOR OF MICROSYSTEM ENGINEERING AND MECHANO-INFORMATICS, NAGOYA UNIVERSITY, JAPAN
- **2045** — RICHARD S. WALLACE, PROFESSOR OF ELECTRICAL ENGINEERING AND COMPUTER SCIENCE, LEHIGH UNIVERSITY

2000 2002 2004 2005 2006 2008 2010 2012 2014 2015 2016 2018 **2019** 2020 2022 2024 2026 2028 2030 2032 2034 2036 2038 2040 2042 2044 2045

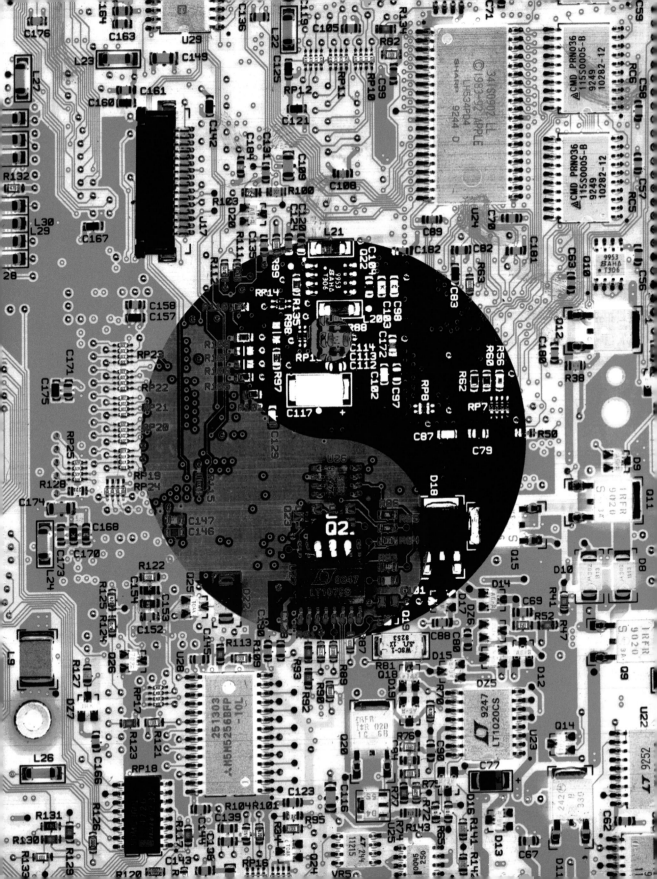

INTEROPERABLE OBJECTS

For some time now interoperable objects have been more than the talk of Silicon Valley; they've almost become marketing gospel at software companies like Autodesk, the world's sixth-largest software company.

Interoperable objects refers to a business strategy – and, more importantly, a programming mandate – that allows users to, for instance, couple one manufacturer's search function with another's word processor. Think of it as a "parts is parts" paradigm for software and operating systems that will solve – finally – the bane of all computer collaborations: incompatibility.

According to the experts we consulted, we are definitely moving closer to a day when most applications will be constructed from interoperable objects. David Vaskevitch points out that with current and proposed object-oriented programming standards, "this is already happening much more in real life than people realize."

Richard Mark Soley agrees: "A surprisingly large number of applications developers have over the years committed to a set of bottom-line interoperability specifications," such as Lotus's WKS file format, which allows applications to exchange text and graphics formats. However, Curtis Yarvin dissents, arguing that because code is idiosyncratic, most of the world's software will remain incompatible.

Interoperable Objects: Laying the foundation for distributed-object computing: A 1994 paper by Mark Betz. *www.ddj.com/ddj/1994/1994.10/betz.htm* American Committee for Interoperable Systems: Homepage for a volunteer organization comprised of 30 companies that looks for ways to ensure "a balance between rewards for innovation and interoperability." *www.sun.com/ACIS/* Introducing Interoperable Objects. *nswt.tuwien.ac.at:8000/se/articles/interopobjects.html* Objects Destined for the Enterprise: Report on Common Object Request Broker Architecture, COBRA, an alternative to Microsoft's Object Linkage and Embedding, OLE, approach. *www.mmt.bme.hu/~kiss/docs/corba/swol-og.html* Thinking Machines Corporation: True parallel computing on the Sun Ultra Workstation. *www.think.com/*

DAVID VASKEVITCH, DIRECTOR OF ENTERPRISE COMPUTING, MICROSOFT CORPORATION

SCOTT BROWN, MANAGER, ADVANCED FILE SYSTEMS, NOVELL, INC.

DANNY HILLIS, FOUNDER, THINKING MACHINES CORPORATION

RICHARD MARK SOLEY, VICE PRESIDENT AND TECHNICAL DIRECTOR, OBJECT MANAGEMENT GROUP, INC.

DEREK LEEBAERT, ADJUNCT PROFESSOR, GRADUATE SCHOOL OF BUSINESS, GEORGETOWN UNIVERSITY, AND EDITOR, *THE FUTURE OF SOFTWARE*

CURTIS YARVIN, LANGUAGE ARCHITECT, XAOS TOOLS, INC.

| 1994 | 1996 | 1998 | 2000 | 2002 | 2004 | 2005 | 2005 | 2005 | 2006 | 2008 | 2010 | 2012 | 2014 | 2015 | 2016 | 2018 | **2019** | 2020 | 2022 | 2024 | 2026 | 2028 | 2030 | 2032 | 2050 | UNLIKELY |

BOTTOM LINE: INTEROPERABLE OBJECTS, THE "INTERCHANGEABLE PARTS" OF THE DIGITAL AGE, WILL HAVE SUCCEEDED IN MINIMIZING INCOMPATIBILITY BY 2019.

105

HUMANS ON MARS

2020

Ever since the days of the ancient Sumerians, some of the world's most brilliant minds have studied and contributed to astronomy, mathematics, and physics, with the hope of one day sending human intelligence throughout the universe. Mars, in particular, has been a focal point of speculation. Countless times in cartoons and sitcoms we have visited Mars and been visited by Martians. Now, say our experts, we are nearing the day when humans will set foot on Mars and perhaps even establish a colony.

Of course, ever since the first close-up images of Mars reached Earth from Mariner 4 (July 1965), we've known that the likelihood of having Martian visitors is next to nil. (Mariner 4 remains adrift in space, some 29 million miles from Earth, having run out of fuel after three years in flight.) Subsequent unmanned visits to Mars have provided often-surprising results

(the discovery of traces of primitive organic compounds), but none that suggest that intelligent life resides on the planet named for the Roman god of war.

With or without a Martian welcoming committee, a man or a woman will likely walk on Mars in the next 40 years, approximately 75 years after Wernher von Braun published an abstract from the first engineering study on the feasibility of a manned flight to Mars.

Timothy Ferris imagines astronauts making a "hit and run" mission to Mars in 2030, and he envisions by 2044 the establishment of a permanent colony that might well be shaped by the experience gained in Biosphere 2 in Arizona. James Oberg, who expects a human touchdown on Mars in 2020, says we will probably first land on Phobos, one of the red planet's moons.

Not surprisingly, our astronomers felt that politics and economics will play a greater role than science in deciding when humans set foot on Mars.

Human Mars Exploration • Detailed of Progressing!: A paper by Douglas A. O'Handley & O Hanmity of Mars. cmex-www.arc.nasa.gov/MarsNews/94q4q_text.html cmex • center for Mars Exploration: A helpful, one-stop reference for human knowledge of Mars. Includes info on previous missions and resources for science teachers. cmex-www.arc .nasa.gov/ Mariner 4 Anniversary Marks 30 Years of Mars Exploration. www.jpl.nasa.gov-80/releases/mars30.html Mars Surveyor Program Description: Homepage to an ambitious enterprise for the exploration of Mars in the next decade. esther.la.asu.edu/asu_tes/TES_Editor/MARS_SURVEYOR/msurvsquyres_descript.html The Planetary Society: Excellent overview of initiatives and trivia. A site for the astronomy hobbyist. wea.mankato.mn.us/tps/index.html

LOU FRIEDMAN, EXECUTIVE DIRECTOR, PLANETARY SOCIETY

DAVID MORRISON, CHIEF OF SPACE SCIENCE DIVISION, NASA-AMES RESEARCH CENTER, AND SCIENCE WRITER

JAMES OBERG, SPACE ENGINEER AND AUTHOR

TIMOTHY FERRIS, AUTHOR OF *THE MIND'S SKY*, AND EMERITUS PROFESSOR OF JOURNALISM, UNIVERSITY OF CALIFORNIA, BERKELEY

2000 2002 2004 2006 2008 2010 2012 2014 2016 2018 **2020** 2020 2022 2024 2026 2028 2030 2032 2034 2036 2038 2040 2042 2044 2046 2048 2050

"SOBER UP" DRUG

2020

Whether it's to ensure a safe drive home from a party or to prevent a hangover the day after, consumer interest in a tablet that quickly brings on sobriety seems assured. As Timothy Leary said wistfully, "Sunday morning wouldn't be too early for the invention of this drug."

According to Michael Aldrich, learning how to reverse the effects of alcohol could be either as simple as discovering the neurochemical basis of alcohol's intoxicating effects, or as complicated as parsing the combined effects of amount, setting, and frequency of alcohol use, and the genetics of the drinker. John Morgan agrees that the problem is finding the correct cell receptors or membranes that mediate intoxication.

Understanding the chemistry would be only the first hurdle, however, as the approval of any drug that promised to reverse inebriation would require a series of rigorous clinical trials. Only then could its widespread availability further encourage all manner of bad behavior before it's time to "sober up" for the drive home.

The Alcohol Neutralizer: A product of herbs and glandulars that helps "safeguard" against alcohol's toxic effects. www.entrepreneurs.net/vye/atcohol.htm
Intoximeters Inc. – Alcohol and the Human Body: Fairly "dry" background on alcohol and its effects. www.intox.com/Physiology.html Alcohol: A chemical analysis of what we drink down. www.calyx.com/~mariolap/sub/alcohol.html Functional Requirements for Chemical Detoxification: Medical information on avoiding harm from alcohol. www.envprevhealthctratl.com/fr-cd.htm Liver – Herbal Formula No. 58: Homepage for a commercial product that helps the body's own detoxifier. www.vitawise.com/herb58.htm

TIMOTHY LEARY, PH.D., PHILOSOPHER

ALEXANDER SHULGIN, M.D., CHEMIST/PHARMACOLOGIST, UNIVERSITY OF CALIFORNIA, BERKELEY, AND CO-AUTHOR OF *PIHKAL: A CHEMICAL LOVE STORY*

JOHN MORGAN, M.D., PROFESSOR OF PHARMACOLOGY, CITY UNIVERSITY OF NEW YORK AND MEMBER OF THE ADVISORY BOARD OF THE DRUG POLICY FOUNDATION

ANDREW WEIL, M.D., AUTHOR OF *SPONTANEOUS HEALING AND NATURAL HEALTH, NATURAL MEDICINE*

MICHAEL ALDRICH, PH.D., CURATOR, FITZ HUGH LUDLOW MEMORIAL LIBRARY

1990 1992 1994 1996 1998 2000 2002 2004 2006 2008 2009 2010 2012 2014 2016 2018 **2020** 2022 2024 2026 2028 2030 2032 2034 2036 2050 2050

COMMERCIALLY VIABLE MAGNETIC LEVITATION TRAINS IN THE UNITED STATES

2021

Some U.S. engineers and a fair number of U.S. travelers have watched with envy as Germany, Japan, and France have designed, developed, and run high-speed trains. Who could blame anyone sitting in bumper-to-bumper traffic for daydreaming about a 200 mile-per-hour commute between Wall Street and New Haven, Burbank and San Diego?

For years now Americans have all but given up on their railways, even as airports and freeways became increasingly congested with traffic. Among the rail projects the U.S. government aborted was the development and implementation of magnetic levitation (mag-lev) technology, first demonstrated in 1966 by James Powell and Gordon Danby. Mag-lev uses magnetic force to suspend and propel a vehicle several inches above a guiding rail. The Germans and Japanese have developed two different types of mag-lev technology. Oversimplifying a bit, the German electromagnetic system (which is closest to commercialization) takes advantage of magnetic attraction, whereas the Japanese superconducting model propels the vehicle by utilizing a repulsive force resulting from repeated reversals in the polarity of the two elements. As Peter H. Stone reported in a 1992 article for *The American Prospect,* "To date, both [Japan and Germany] have provided about a billion dollars to develop commercial prototypes that float along guideways at speeds approaching 300 miles per hour."

The German and Japanese attempts to institute high-speed mag-lev service are almost certainly inevitable – and likely profitable. The conventional, steel-wheeled Japanese bullet trains on the Tokyo – Osaka line took only 18 months to pay back their construction costs (US$640 million). Whether Americans should develop their own mag-lev technology remains the subject of some debate, but in 1991 the U.S. government did commit to producing a prototype by allocating US$725 million for its development.

Among the experts we consulted, Richard L. Klimisch thinks the Japanese type of mag-lev trains could be commercially viable if superconductors that operate at room temperature can be developed. However, Rupert Welch and Thomas B. Deen agree that mag-lev trains don't create sufficient advantages over high-speed, steel-wheel trains to justify their cost. As a result, they see a commercial mag-lev line in the United States only if the government continues to subsidize its development, and then only if the project can convince voters of its ability to reduce traffic problems and pollution, and to facilitate two conversions: defense-industry jobs into mag-lev infrastructure jobs, and old railway tracks into mag-lev lines.

Sandia National Laboratories: Homepage of an engineering firm that produces technology enabling trains to reach speeds of 200+ miles per hour. *www.sandia.gov/pulspowr/ppeng/seraphim.html* The Faster Track, Should We Build a High-Speed Rail System?: An essay by Peter H. Stone on whether the United States should build high-speed rail networks like those found in Japan, France, and Germany. *epn.org/prospect/11/11ston.html* The Aerodynamic Design of High Speed MAGLEV Vehicles Using MDO Design Methodology: A gallery of mag-lev vehicles capable of speeds of 300 mph. *www.aoe.vt.edu/mad/articles/MAGLEV.html* PeoplePod™ Infopage: A mag-lev concept sketched and introduced by Aerovisions, Inc. of California. *weber.u.washington.edu/~jbs/pod.htm*

RICHARD L. KLIMISCH, PH.D., VICE PRESIDENT OF ENGINEERING, AMERICAN AUTOMOBILE MANUFACTURERS ASSOCIATION

THOMAS B. DEEN, EXECUTIVE DIRECTOR, TRANSPORTATION RESEARCH BOARD

NOAH RIFKIN, DIRECTOR OF TECHNOLOGY DEPLOYMENT, UNITED STATES DEPARTMENT OF TRANSPORTATION

RUPERT WELCH, EDITOR, *INSIDE DOT AND TRANSPORTATION WEEK*

STEVEN E. SHLADOVER, ACTING DIRECTOR, CALIFORNIA PARTNERS FOR ADVANCED TRANSIT AND HIGHWAYS

2000 2002 2004 2006 2008 2010 2010 2012 2014 2015 2016 2018 2020 **2021** 2022 2024 2026 2028 2030 2032 2034 2036 2038 2040 2042 2050 NEVER

BOTTOM LINE: BECAUSE THE U.S. GOVERNMENT DROPPED MAG-LEV DEVELOPMENT IN 1975 AND ONLY RECENTLY BEGAN TO SUBSIDIZE A PROTOTYPE, DON'T LOOK FOR COMMERCIAL, HIGH-SPEED MAG-LEV SERVICE IN THE UNITED STATES BEFORE 2021.

ENTIRELY EX UTERO FETAL DEVELOPMENT

2022

URLS/FURTHER READING

IVF – GIFT, ZIFT and ICSI: The fertilization services available at the University of California, San Francisco (UCSF). www.ihr.com/ucsfivf/ivf/ivf/gift.html Embryo and Semen Freezing: More from UCSF, specifically on their ability to preserve embryos and sperm. www.ihr.com/ucsfivf/embfreez.html Ethics of Embryo Research: An article by Ronald M. Green of *The Washington Post* raises a few difficult questions. solar.rtd.utk.edu/news/washington/research/9410/9410-3.html ZyGen Laboratory: Lab services in Los Angeles County and who they serve best. www.zygen.com/coinfo.htm#other

"The enormous room on the ground floor faced towards the north. Cold for all the summer beyond the panes, for all the tropical heat of the room itself, a harsh thin light glared through the windows, hungrily seeking some draped lay figure, some pallid shape of academic goose-flesh, but finding only the glass and nickel and bleakly shining porcelain of a laboratory. Wintriness responded to wintriness. The overalls of the workers were white, their hands gloved with a pale of corpse-coloured rubber. The light was frozen, dead, a ghost. Only from the yellow barrels of the microscopes did it borrow a certain rich and living substance, lying along the polished tubes like butter, streak after luscious streak in long recession down the work tables.

"'And this,' said the Director opening the door, 'is the Fertilizing Room.'"

These lines, written by Aldous Huxley in 1931 in *Brave New World*, introduce readers to a terrifying world in which the same system of controls corporations use to mass-produce commodities has been applied to mass-producing human life. Over 60 years later, much of the technology required to create a society like Huxley's has arrived. Fortunately, however, these advances have thus far been utilized to begin or preserve life and not by the State to control it.

In 1977, scientists at Bourne Hall at Cambridge University, England, performed the first in vitro fertilization, a procedure whereby eggs that have been removed from a woman's ovary are fertilized by sperm outside the body. Since 1977, tens of thousands of in vitro fertilizations have been performed to overcome various types of infertility and have given rise to several other techniques, including GIFT (gamete intrafallopian transfer), ZIFT (zygote intrafallopian transfer), and ICSI, (intracytoplasmic sperm injection). Developed and first demonstrated at the University of California, San Francisco in 1994, (the first child produced by this method was born in February 1995), ICSI involves injecting a single sperm into the center of a human egg.

As for technology sustaining fetal development outside the body, incubators can now support extremely young infants (little more than 20 weeks of age) born prematurely or rescued from the womb of an injured mother. Medical science, in other words, is narrowing the gap between test-tube conception and machine-assisted development, and may well have closed it completely by 2022.

Looking out for future children, Nancie S. Martin jokes, "it would be so nice to avoid all that muss and fuss, but who are you going to blame in therapy if you don't have parents?"

RICHARD KADREY, EDITOR OF *COVERT CULTURE SOURCEBOOK*, AND AUTHOR OF *KAMIKAZE L'AMOUR*

NANCIE S. MARTIN, PRESIDENT OF JOUISANCE PRODUCTIONS AND FORMER EDITOR OF *PLAYGIRL*

HOWARD RHEINGOLD, AUTHOR OF *VIRTUAL COMMUNITY, VIRTUAL REALITY* AND EDITOR OF *THE MILLENNIUM WHOLE EARTH CATALOG*

ISADORA ALMAN, "ASK ISADORA" SYNDICATED COLUMNIST, AND SEX AND RELATIONSHIP COUNSELOR

TRICORDER

2023

URLS/FURTHER READING

I-STAT Corporation: Homepage of a device that can do some, if not all, of what a tricorder supposedly does. *www.i-stat.com/* Hewlett-Packard: Announcement about a less expensive, noninvasive sensor used to monitor blood-oxygen levels. *www.hp.com/pressrel/oct95/3ooct95a.html*

Star Trek's Dr. Leonard H. "Bones" McCoy made diagnosis look easy. The Starship *Enterprise*'s chief medical officer with the country-doctor demeanor dug quickly into his satchel and whipped out his trusty tricorder. Then, passing it over his patient's body at spray-painting distance, he knew in a flash the patient's vital signs and the nature and severity of any internal injuries he or she may have suffered.

The appeal and fame of the fictional *Star Trek* biosign monitor aside, the medical experts we consulted disagree about the value and feasibility of such a device. Dr. Richard Satava says that prototypes already exist, noting that U.S. Army Rangers will wear personal status monitors, or PSMs, during training exercises this year. As Satava tells it, the PSMs transmit a soldier's vital signs and location to a remote command post via satellite. Satava predicts that civilian versions of the devices will be available within five years.

"We've had a tricorder for years," scoffs Dr. David Vining. "It's called 'feeling for a pulse.'" Vining says the tricorder is "far-fetched" and imagines instead a device or combination of devices that perform similar functions, such as a stethoscope with a portable ultrasound scanner, or a device that screens body fluids, like the one that tests saliva for HIV (now in development). "What I *can* foresee," Vining jokes, "is a tricorder that tells physicians if the patient is fully insured or not."

RICHARD SATAVA, M.D., PROGRAM MANAGER, ADVANCED BIOMEDICAL TECHNOLOGY, ADVANCED RESEARCH PROJECTS AGENCY

ANTHONY DIGIOIA III, M.D., CO-DIRECTOR, CENTER FOR MEDICAL ROBOTICS AND COMPUTER-ASSISTED SURGERY, CARNEGIE MELLON UNIVERSITY

DAVID VINING, M.D., ASSISTANT PROFESSOR OF ABDOMINAL IMAGING, BOWMAN GRAY SCHOOL OF MEDICINE, WAKE FOREST UNIVERSITY

PHILIP GREEN, M.D., PRESIDENT, TELESURGICAL CORPORATION

1998 2000 2002 2004 2006 2008 2010 2012 2014 2016 2018 2020 2022 **2023** 2024 2026 2028 2030 2032 2034 2036 2038 2040 2042 2044 2050 NEVER

BOTTOM LINE: IT WILL LIKELY BE 2023 BEFORE ANYONE HAS A TRICORDER PER SE, BUT OTHER HANDY DIAGNOSTIC INSTRUMENTS THAT WORK ON CONTACT WITH A PATIENT WILL ARRIVE MUCH SOONER.

CONTACT WITH EXTRATERRESTRIAL INTELLIGENCE

2025

Abductees Anonymous: An online magazine and support group for those wishing to share their abduction experience. www.cyberdate.com/~uJonline/ extra-Terrestrial Exposure Law: An article, complete with the language of the law, on the legislation that makes it illegal for U.S. citizens to come in contact with an extraterrestrial. www.cs.bgsu.edu/~jzawodn/ufo/et-law.html SETI League: Homepage of the educational and scientific nonprofit devoted to scanning the heavens. seti.setileague.org/homepg.html UFO Sightings by Astronauts: Testimonies of 13 astronauts. www.cs.bgsu.edu/~jzawodn/ufo/astro-sightings.html Institute for the Study of Contact with Non-human Intelligence: New Age meets science fiction in this publication/catalog. www.catalog.com/cgibin/var/demniso/index.html

Particles from Mars, borne on asteroids traveling through our solar system, are already "in contact" with the Earth, but contact between intelligent extraterrestial life and humans remains the controversial claim of a few – and a stimulating, perhaps even slightly terrifying, prospect for the rest of us.

If you are skeptical about reports of alien abduction, and therefore doubt that contact has already been achieved, then you likely agree with the experts we consulted, who say that the day human/alien contact occurs is nearly impossible to predict. "Any guess," says Lou Friedman, "is a statement of faith." Nevertheless, James Oberg asserts that by 2026 "the extraterrestrial origin of some already-noticed artifact [on earth] will be generally accepted."

Building faith in the inevitablity of a human/extraterrestrial dialogue is one function of SETI (search for extraterrestrial intelligence) programs, which were initiated by NASA and originally funded by Congress, and have since secured private funding. Discussing the likelihood of a "close encounter of the third kind," Timothy Ferris maintains that our search of the heavens will continue to teach us about ourselves, whether we find something or somebody out there or not. If we do encounter a more intelligent life form, he suggests, we will probably be as inscrutable to them as we are to dogs.

Amazingly, establishing contact with extraterrestrials is currently a federal crime. Title 14, Section 1211 of the Code of Federal Regulations, adopted on July 16, 1969, makes it illegal for U.S. citizens to have an encounter with extraterrestrials or their vehicles. Those found guilty of such an encounter face quarantine (with or without a hearing), up to a year in prison, and a fine of US$5,000.

As those who oppose it point out, the law will not so much prevent contact as silence witnesses.

TIMOTHY FERRIS, AUTHOR OF *THE MIND'S SKY*, AND EMERITUS PROFESSOR OF JOURNALISM, UNIVERSITY OF CALIFORNIA, BERKELEY

JAMES OBERG, SPACE ENGINEER AND AUTHOR

DAVID MORRISON, CHIEF OF SPACE SCIENCE DIVISION, NASA-AMES RESEARCH CENTER, AND SCIENCE WRITER

LOU FRIEDMAN, EXECUTIVE DIRECTOR, PLANETARY SOCIETY

〈ATOM〉*

*〈TRANSLATED FROM
THE JAPANESE〉

2029

FURTHER READING

Foresight Institute: The journal of a nonprofit group preparing the world for nanotech. A nanotech reader. *www.foresight.org* The Incredible Shrinking World of Eric Drexler: Anthony B. Perkins interviews Drexler for *Red Herring* magazine. *www.herring.com/mag/issue22/world.html* W. M. Keck Center for Molecular Electronics: Bulletin from one of the leading academic research facilities (at Syracuse University). *www.ecs.syr.edu/keck/keck.html* Center for Nanoscale Science and Technology: "A message for prospective students" of nanotech, furnished by Rice University. *cnst.rice.edu/*

One of the many dreams born of research in nanotechnology (see "Commercially Viable Nanotechnology," page 39) is the ability to deploy inside the human body mechanical agents so tiny they could travel unfelt within the bloodstream and even effect cell repair at the molecular level.

Building such a miniscule machine, observes K. Eric Drexler, is an enormously complex engineering task, but one that might be possible with the help of artificial intelligence. By this he means that the nanometer-sized agent could be programmed, much as bots are today (see "Intelligent Agents," page 7), to detect its target, react to certain chemical cues, and, like a cell, clone itself so that enough "mechanics" are present to finish the repair job.

Donald W. Brenner, however, says that "repairing a cell as one would repair a car – using mechanical forces – is surely not the way to go." A better approach, he believes, would augment natural chemical processes with "a specially designed vehicle that would selectively deliver chemical reagents to a cell." Similarly, the cell-repair machine that Richard E. Smalley envisions will not build cell structures atom by atom but will instead be protein-based.

As J. Storrs Hall points out, there's already a natural model for cell therapy that is more sophisticated than nanotechnology: viruses. Hall predicts they will remain ahead of nanotech in their ability to remodel cells.

RICHARD E. SMALLEY, PH.D., PROFESSOR OF CHEMISTRY AND PHYSICS, RICE UNIVERSITY, AND CHIEF INVESTIGATOR OF RICE'S CENTER FOR NANOSCALE SCIENCE AND TECHNOLOGY

K. ERIC DREXLER, PH.D., CHAIRMAN, FORESIGHT INSTITUTE, AND AUTHOR OF *ENGINES OF CREATION: THE COMING ERA OF NANOTECHNOLOGY*

ROBERT R. BIRGE, PH.D., DISTINGUISHED PROFESSOR OF CHEMISTRY, AND DIRECTOR OF THE W. M. KECK CENTER FOR MOLECULAR ELECTRONICS, SYRACUSE UNIVERSITY

DONALD W. BRENNER, PH.D., ASSOCIATE PROFESSOR, DEPARTMENT OF MATERIALS SCIENCE AND ENGINEERING, NORTH CAROLINA STATE UNIVERSITY

J. STORRS HALL, PH.D., COMPUTER SCIENTIST, RUTGERS UNIVERSITY, AND MODERATOR, SCI.NANOTECHNOLOGY USENET GROUP

2000　2002　2004　2006　2008　2010　2012　2014　2016　2018　2020　2022　2024　2026　2028　**2029**　2030　2032　2034　2035　2036　2038　2040　2042　2044　2046　2050

BOTTOM LINE: BECAUSE CELLULAR REPAIR WILL REQUIRE NANOTECHNOLOGY THAT REMAINS HIGHLY THEORETICAL, DON'T EXPECT TO PUT MOLECULAR

MORE THAN 50 PERCENT DRIVE ELECTRIC CARS

2034

The long litany of ills internal combustion engines visit upon us – automobile emissions, for example, are the source of half of all urban smog in the United States – is one reason why electric cars continue to hold promise for the future. Who doesn't want to drive to the beach safe in the knowledge they aren't polluting the air above an entire coastal region?

Understanding why electric cars remain a novelty – various sources estimate that only 2,000 to 3,000 currently ply U.S. streets – is really no great feat. Until recently, the range of most electric cars was extremely limited; they perform (accelerate, for example) well below their gas-guzzling cousins; they cost too much (generally twice as much as conventional cars); and their development has not been a priority for some 90 years.

These conditions, say the experts we consulted, are slowly changing. Electric cars, which constituted 38 percent of the automobile market at the turn of the 20th century, are staging a gradual comeback thanks to technical advances largely spurred by governmental action. In noting the importance of instituting and enforcing governmental action in advancing cleaner modes of transportation, our experts applauded California's Zero-Emission Vehicle mandate, which requires that by 1998 at least 2 percent of all cars manufactured in California emit no pollutants.

Still, our experts acknowledge the car companies' complaint that the batteries and other energy-storage devices needed to make electric cars truly competitive have yet to be developed. Until electric cars have greater range than the current 70 miles or so per charge, cost-reducing mass production of these vehicles will be delayed. Given these range limitations, Richard L. Klimisch thinks electric cars will be practical for city use only.

Finally, there's the view of skeptics like Rupert Welch. Welch thinks battery-powered cars will not be needed for pollution reduction because "air standards could be reached today by getting older cars off the road."

URLS/FURTHER READING

Eco-Motion: Complete yellow pages and bibliography of developers of electric vehicles. halycon.com/slough/ecomotion Electric Cars U.S.A.: Article by Jim Motavalli from *E* magazine provides useful overview and plenty of detail, circa 1994. www.dc.enews.com/magazines/e/archive/1994/060294.2.html Green Wheels: Info on conversions of existing fossil-fuel burners to electric cars. northshore.shore.net/~kester/gwhome.html Solectria: Homepage of the self-proclaimed leader in electric vehicle (EV) tech. www.solectria.com/

2000
2002
2004
2006
2008

2010 NOAH RIFKIN, DIRECTOR OF TECHNOLOGY DEPLOYMENT, UNITED STATES DEPARTMENT OF TRANSPORTATION
2012
2014
2016
2018
2020
2022
2024
2025 THOMAS B. DEEN, EXECUTIVE DIRECTOR, TRANSPORTATION RESEARCH BOARD
2026
2028
2030
2032
2034 RUPERT WELCH, EDITOR, *INSIDE DOT AND TRANSPORTATION WEEK*
2036
2038
2040 STEVEN E. SHLADOVER, ACTING DIRECTOR, CALIFORNIA PARTNERS FOR ADVANCED TRANSIT AND HIGHWAYS
2042
2044
2046
2050
UNLIKELY RICHARD L. KLIMISCH, PH.D., VICE PRESIDENT OF ENGINEERING, AMERICAN AUTOMOBILE MANUFACTURERS ASSOCIATION

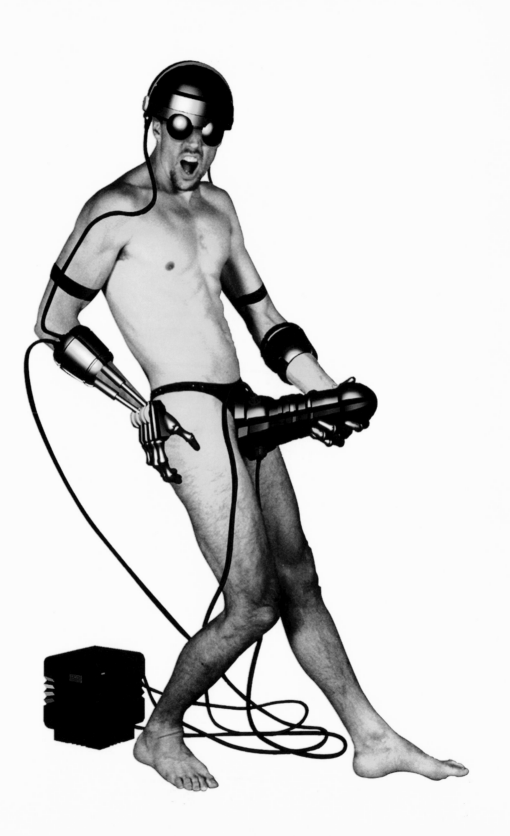

In 1974 Theodor Nelson coined the term *dildonics* to refer to an instrument that used sonic impulses to stimulate tactilely the body's erogenous zones. Years later the term lends itself readily to sex experienced through a computer interface and the hype that now surrounds what is termed *teledildonics* has all but drowned out discussion of the myriad other applications of VR.

The idea is this: wearing 3-D goggles and a body suit snug as a condom and with thousands of what Howard Rheingold calls "intelligent sensor-effectors" that reproduce the sensation of a lover's touch, a person could experience sex with someone else likewise suited up or at the controls of a computer program that activates the sensors.

Unfortunately, the basic transducer and feedback technology necessary for teledildonics, our experts say, won't be available until most of us old enough to read this are octogenarians; even then, they speculate, it will be embraced by some but not by all. (See also "Virtual Sex Slave," page 133).

Nancie S. Martin suggests that the first wave of teledildonics will likely be some sort of MIDI-controlled vibrator or suction machine (see "Orgasmatron," page 77), while Isadora Alman says that in at least one sense, teledildonics are already here. Defining teledildonics more broadly as technologies that arouse and give pleasure from a distance, she notes that couples today can purchase battery-powered vibrators that can be remote-controlled. "You could agree with a partner to wear or secrete them under your clothes at a party," Alman giggles, "and when you see them talking to someone cute, give them a little buzz to remind them of you."

FURTHER READING

VR Bodysuit: A prototype. *www.prairienet.org/~vrsuit/adsl.html* Tactile Dialogue: A discussion on our emergent visual/multimedia culture with a reference to CyberSM & Cybersex. *www.khm.uni-koeln.de/~kwolf/Tactile.html* Telenor: Homepage of company investigating ways to access virtual worlds. *www.fou.telenor.no/televr/* CyberSM & Cybersex. *www.khm.uni-koeln.de/~kwolf/Tactile.html* Telenor: Homepage of company investigating ways to access virtual worlds. *www.fou.telenor.no/televr/*

ISADORA ALMAN, "ASK ISADORA" SYNDICATED COLUMNIST, AND SEX AND RELATIONSHIP COUNSELORR

NANCIE S. MARTIN, PRESIDENT OF JOUISANCE PRODUCTIONS AND FORMER EDITOR OF *PLAYGIRL*

RICHARD KADREY, EDITOR, *COVERT CULTURE SOURCEBOOK*, AND AUTHOR OF *KAMIKAZE L'AMOUR*

HOWARD RHEINGOLD, AUTHOR OF *VIRTUAL COMMUNITY*, *VIRTUAL REALITY* AND EDITOR OF *THE MILLENNIUM WHOLE EARTH CATALOG*

FIRST CRYONIC REANIMATION

2043

It's a desire as old as life, and among some cryonicists it's a rallying cry: "Abolish Mortality!"

Here's what they envision: One day you die (or de-animate, as the advocates say), and over the next few days, technicians slowly but surely freeze either your head or entire body, eventually submerging what's left of you in liquid nitrogen (-196 degrees Celsius). Then, years from now, you are brought back to life. Disoriented at first, memories soon remind you of who you are. By that time, advanced surgical techniques have reversed the effects of freezer burn on your gray matter and have jump-started stalled metabolic processes (see "Cell Repair Technology," page 119). You undergo extensive physical therapy in an effort to adjust to your new body – one that has been cloned for you from your own DNA. Welcome to a brave new world where the Big Chill no longer means death and where true death occurs only when the DNA needed to construct new tissue has been destroyed.

Cryonics, the latest and arguably most promising technology yet for achieving longevity, is the science of deep-freezing tissue before it has begun to decay with an eye toward reanimating it later. The term dates to 1965 and Robert C. W. Ettinger's book, *The Prospect of Immortality*. Interestingly, as early as 1773 Benjamin Franklin considered the possibility of "a method of embalming drowned persons, in such a manner that they may be recalled to life at any period, however distant."

At least four companies make good on Ettinger's idea, insofar as we have the front-end (deep-freezing) technology today and can theoretically keep someone frozen until we have the back-end (reviving) technology. In fact, as this book went to press, these four organizations were maintaining 67 heads and/or bodies in cryosuspension. Alcor Foundation, perhaps the best known of the four, sustains 13 whole body and 19 neuro (head) suspensions. (Walt Disney's body and head, by the way, are not among them. His cryosuspension is an urban myth.)

Far-fetched as cryonics strikes some, it is, according to Ralph C. Merkle, "feasible in principle, if not yet in practice." Already, he and others note, kidneys and other internal organs have been frozen and later restored to their functions. The trick, he says, will be to revive a brain – with the memory intact. "Within ten years," says Steve Bridge optimistically, "we'll know how memory functions well enough to see if particular structures that are vital to it have survived."

To reach that point, says Art Quaife, will require investment in R & D. Quaife points to recent interest from Wall Street in "spin-off" cryonic technologies like BioTime's blood substitute (which, in the context of cryonics, could serve as a biological antifreeze); to advances in cloning (lizards are already cloned in labs); and to the ability to repair tissue damaged by ice crystals.

Significantly, our experts suggest that the reanimation of people currently in cryonic suspension may not be the best measure of this technology. Instead, they point to cryogenic medicine as a better indicator of progress in cryonics. Imagine, says Merkle, "being able to operate on a person as a mechanic does a car – to turn off the motor completely, fix what is wrong, and then turn it back on again."

ART QUAIFE, PH.D., PRESIDENT OF TRANSTIME

STEVE BRIDGE, PRESIDENT, ALCOR LIFE EXTENSION FOUNDATION

CHARLES PLATT, VICE PRESIDENT AND CO-FOUNDER, CRYO-CARE FOUNDATION

RALPH C. MERKLE, PH.D., DIRECTOR OF NANOTECHOLOGY RESEARCH, XEROX PARC

2000 2005 2010 2015 2020 2025 2030 2035 2040 **2043** 2045 2046 2050 2050 2055 2060 2065 2070 2075 2080 2085 2090 2095 2100 2105 2110 2115

Matic Storage Unit: Homepage of a manufacturer of the dewars where cryosuspended persons are kept. 147.252.134.2/icc/cryogenic.html BioPreservation, Inc.: www.widemedia.com/annual/cryonics.html CryoNet: Introduction with "Is it for you?" questionnaire. www.c2.org:80/-kqb/cryonet.html Cryo-Cell Ireland Ltd./Uni-
Homepage of one cryoservice provider. www.webcom.com/~cryocare/bpi/bpi.html Alcor Foundation: Homepage of the leading cryoservice provider.
www.webcom.com/~alcor/ Cryo-Care: Another cryoservice provider. www.cryocare.org/cryocare/

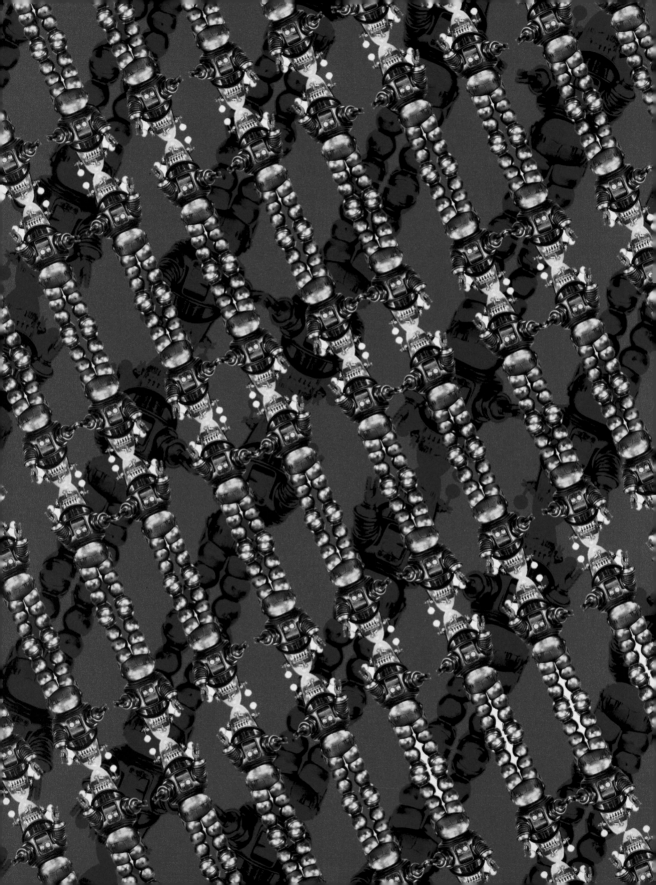

SELF-REPLICATING ROBOT

2044

Fantasy applications for nanotechnology abound, but perhaps none excites more interest or controversy than visions of a swarm of nanoscale robots that replicate themselves and enable physical objects to change their shape or color. (See also "Commercially Viable Nanotechnology," page 39 and "Cell Repair Technology," page 119.) For example, futurists at Rutgers University envision a "Utility Fog" of self-replicating robots which, when painted on a wall, could change to a different color every day, or when applied to an avant-garde coffee table could reconfigure it into a Queen Anne piece. But robots need not be microscopic to be self-replicating, and studies by NASA suggest that the first application of a self-replicating robot will not likely be to alter an object's molecular structure, but instead to explore outer space.

If the idea of an inorganic structure capable of reproducing itself is difficult to get your mind around, Joe Engleberger can help. Discounting the prospects for self-replicating nanorobots, he reminds us that on many kinds of assembly lines robots already assemble other machines, including other robots. Meanwhile, to understand further how machines could make themselves, we can turn to the theoretical work of John von Neumann, which established that robot replication might rely on only two elements: a universal computer, a program that serves as the blueprint or DNA for the new robots, and a universal constructor, a machine that carries out the universal computer's instructions.

Perhaps predictably, most of our experts agree that the biggest obstacles facing development of self-replicating robots are not technical but financial. Richard S. Wallace cites a 1980 NASA study that, he says, indicates that "self-replicating lunar factories were within range even then." Wallace concedes, however, that no one is knocking down engineers' doors with the billions of dollars of R & D funds needed to build the things. Although Rodney A. Brooks believes that self-replicating nanorobots could be with us in a decade, he suggests that "they will not be as satisfying as the sci-fi vision of self-replicating robots," like the "Utility Fog."

URLS/FURTHER READING
NASA and Self-Replicating Systems: Two works by Ralph C. Merkle on the concept and implications of this nanotechnology. *nano.xerox.com/nanotech/selfRepNASA .html* or *nano.xerox.com/nanotech/selfRepJBIS.html* Utility Fog: "Suppose, instead of building the object you want atom by atom, the tiny robots linked their arms together to form a solid mass in the shape of the object you wanted?" *nanotech.rutgers.edu/nanotech/Ufog.html* Nanotechnology, Self-Reproduction & Agile Manufacturing: A lively introduction by Nick Szabo. *www.digicash.com/~nick/nano.musings.html*

JOHN CANNY, ASSOCIATE PROFESSOR OF COMPUTER SCIENCE, UNIVERSITY OF CALIFORNIA, BERKELEY

RODNEY A. BROOKS, ASSOCIATE DIRECTOR, MIT ARTIFICIAL INTELLIGENCE LABORATORY, AND CHAIR, IS ROBOTICS, INC.

TOSHIO FUKUDA, PROFESSOR OF MICROSYSTEM ENGINEERING AND MECHANO-INFORMATICS, NAGOYA UNIVERSITY, JAPAN

RICHARD S. WALLACE, PROFESSOR OF ELECTRICAL ENGINEERING AND COMPUTER SCIENCE, LEHIGH UNIVERSITY

JOE ENGELBERGER, CHAIR, HELPMATE ROBOTICS, INC.

2000
2005
2010
2013
2015
2020
2025
2030
2035
2040
2044
2045
2050
2055
2060
2065
2070
2075
2080
2085
2090
2095
2100
2105
2110
2115
UNLIKELY

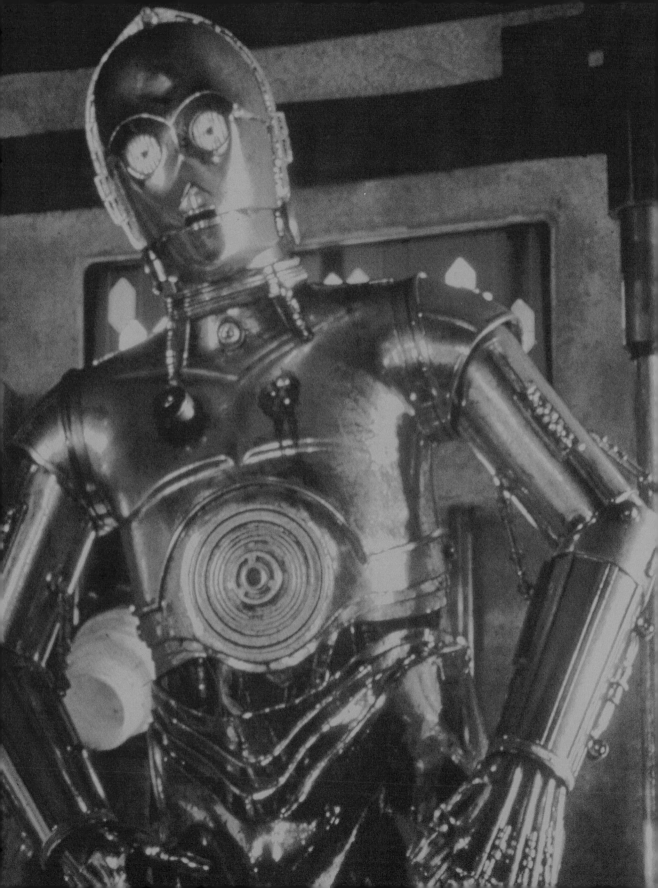

Filmmaker George Lucas might yet live to see the day robots like *Star Wars* "droid" C-3PO walk among us. Still, as fans of *Star Wars* can appreciate, making C-3PO – a humanoid robot that walks, talks, translates languages, generally thinks and acts independent of its creator, and even worries about others – is a tall order.

Even though anthropomorphic robots were the focus of a great deal of sci-fi and futurist hype in the 1950s, research projects in this field have only recently begun at institutions such as MIT and Tokyo University. These efforts are predicated on the idea that if robots are to think and act like humans, they must be physically similar to them as well. "The premise," John Canny explains, is "that virtually all human reasoning, and especially abstract human reasoning, is firmly grounded in three-dimensional and anthropomorphic metaphors."

Several of our experts suggest, however, that humanoid robots be left in Hollywood prop rooms. They say that instead of trying to engineer robots in human likeness, emphasis should be placed on engineering robots that, regardless of their appearance, work well with humans. What is needed, they say, are advances in such technologies as voice recognition, navigation aides, and other sensors that will make users "comfortable" around robots. Joe Engelberger, for one, holds little hope for a C-3PO model, instead envisioning a personal robot that more closely resembles C-3PO's squat pal, the hydrant-like R2D2.

The Courier Robot: A report on a robot practiced in "collision avoidance" with movie demo. *tommyjsc.nasa.gov/er/er4/courer/* Humanoid Autonomous Robot Project: Meet "Chie," a humanoid robot that is the work of several students and faculty at a university in Japan. *www.jsk.t.u-tokyo.ac.jp/research/harp/humanoid.html* MIT Artificial Intelligence (AI) Laboratory: Updates on events and projects at one of the leading centers for AI research. *www.ai.mit.edu/index-text.html* Engineers Abandon Human Models: Getting beyond sci-fi visions of anthropomorphized robots. Well-written, with historical context. *stis.nsf.gov/nsf/homepage/frontier/julaug95/robotics.htm* IS Robotics: Report on a robot developed by a Somerville, MA company. *haifa.isx.com:80/~isr/Racs.html*

TOSHIO FUKUDA, PROFESSOR OF MICROSYSTEM ENGINEERING AND MECHANO-INFORMATICS, NAGOYA UNIVERSITY, JAPAN

RODNEY A. BROOKS, ASSOCIATE DIRECTOR, MIT ARTIFICIAL INTELLIGENCE LABORATORY, AND CHAIR, IS ROBOTICS, INC.

JOHN CANNY, ASSOCIATE PROFESSOR OF COMPUTER SCIENCE, UNIVERSITY OF CALIFORNIA, BERKELEY

RICHARD S. WALLACE, PROFESSOR OF ELECTRICAL ENGINEERING AND COMPUTER SCIENCE, LEHIGH UNIVERSITY

JOE ENGELBERGER, CHAIR, HELPMATE ROBOTICS, INC.

2000 2005 2010 2015 2020 2025 2030 2035 2040 2045 **2047** 2050 2055 2060 2065 2070 2075 2080 2085 2090 2095 2100 2105 2110 2115 2120 UNLIKELY

MOST U.S. PRODUCE GROWN HYDROPONICALLY

2051

Pushed by an ever-expanding world population and pulled by new technologies, food
growers and suppliers have never faced a
greater demand nor had so many potential
ways to fulfill it. One of the options is indoor
hydroponic gardening, which allows crops
to be grown anywhere year-round using a
nutrient-rich water bath instead of soil.

Although few of the experts we consulted
doubt that hydroponics will prove useful, they
disagree on the extent to which it will catch
on. Manfred Kroger, who has been eating
hydroponic lettuce for 20 years, says it will be
2085 before most of our produce is grown
hydroponically. By then, Kroger predicts, we
will have built large-scale hydroponic sky-
scrapers as an answer to the loss of farmland
to suburban sprawl.

Jim McCamant, however, thinks hydroponics
will never take off on a large scale because
"it's always going to be cheaper to use the
nutrients that are already in the ground."

Hydroponic Instruction Package – Hydroponic Systems: An introduction to the five primary hydroponic systems. *www.cals.cornell.edu/dept/education/IMS
/hydrosystems.html* Hydroponic Society of America: Homepage to a major trade organization. *www.intercom.net/user/aquaedu/hsa/index.html* Aloha 'Aina Hydro
Farms Inc.: FAQ from one of the biggest producers of hydroponic tomatoes, lettuce, and cucumbers. *hawaii-shopping.com/~sammonet/hydroveggies.html* SolaDome
Hydroponics: An excellent site for those just getting started. *olis.mtx.net.au/soladome/index.html* History of Hydroponics: A complete history of the field, including
the source of the term. *www.npac.sg-9080/~csk/lecture/l_hist.html*

MAHMOUD EL-BEGEARMI, PH.D., NUTRITION AND FOOD SAFETY SPECIALIST, UNIVERSITY OF MAINE COOPERATIVE EXTENSION

MANFRED KROGER, PH.D., PROFESSOR OF FOOD SCIENCE, PENNSYLVANIA STATE UNIVERSITY

ELLEN MARTIN, SCIENCE COMMUNICATIONS, DNA PLANT TECHNOLOGY

JIM McCAMANT, EDITOR, *AGBIOTECH STOCK LETTER*

1985 1990 1995 2000 2005 2010 2015 2020 2025 2030 2035 2040 2045 2050 **2051** 2055 2060 2065 2070 2075 2080 2085 2090 2095 2100 2105 NEVER

VIRTUAL SEX SLAVE

2055

A digital sex slave – a computer program designed to indulge a computer-user's every desire – would, no doubt, redefine safe sex. Imagine pulling on a fabric wired to a computer and a head-mounted display and seeing and feeling a sex partner that doesn't exist, doesn't have another party controlling it, and does what you ask or tell it to do. Not only would there be no exchange of fluids, but no one would get exploited. Notes Richard Kadrey, in understatement, it "would eliminate certain legal problems if there is no flesh-and-blood sex worker involved."

Ideal as it may sound, the virtual reality technology that could make computer-generated coitus a tactile experience is not yet available – nor, according to our experts, is it likely to be anytime soon. Instead, virtual sex today takes the form of explicit email or chats ("type dirty to me"), computer games like *Virtual Valerie,* or services that reproduce phone sex over the Internet. Using CU-SeeMe videoconferencing, for example, one can now "see and hear" a partner on the World Wide Web, much as one can dial up and have anal sex over the phone.

To bring about sex with a virtual partner that involves more than a keyboard and a monitor will require true teledildonics (see page 123) and significant improvements in real-time virtual reality. Even so, our experts aren't sure digital sex slaves will ever be as ideal as they might seem. Kadrey suggests that even when computer sex comes of age, "it will not resemble ordinary sex at all…. It will be an entirely different form of sexuality, with its own pleasures and pitfalls, fans and adversaries, fetishists and posers. Whether you think this is a good thing or not depends on how you view sexual and body experimentation." As Kadrey notes, "Someone had to be the first person to think of bondage sex. That was a technological and conceptual leap in sexuality. Not everyone thought it was a good idea then and not everyone thinks it's a good idea now, but it exists and is practiced all over the world."

Isadora Alman suggests that role-playing with your current partner might do the trick – and a whole lot sooner. Nancie S. Martin cautions that it would be a mistake to wait for the perfect virtual partner to come along. Says Martin, "Falling in love is already a virtual experience in which you make a real person into a fantasy."

URLS/FURTHER READING
Hot LIVE Sex: New media for the world's oldest profession. www.specdata.com/livesex South Florida's Finest: "She Hears You. You See Her. SHE LOVES IT!" www.specdata.com/livesex/hls_stg.html VideoFantasy: Nude videoconferencing for adults. "No special hardware required." www.videofantasy.com/ Cyber Images Video Phone Sex: Another Web-based watch-and-click sex page. "Watch the girl of your dreams perform live." www.cyberimages.com

ISADORA ALMAN, "ASK ISADORA" SYNDICATED COLUMNIST AND SEX AND RELATIONSHIP COUNSELOR

NANCIE S. MARTIN, PRESIDENT OF JOUISANCE PRODUCTIONS AND FORMER EDITOR OF PLAYGIRL

RICHARD KADREY, EDITOR OF COVERT CULTURE SOURCEBOOK AND AUTHOR OF KAMIKAZE L'AMOUR

HOWARD RHEINGOLD, AUTHOR OF VIRTUAL COMMUNITY, VIRTUAL REALITY AND EDITOR OF THE MILLENNIUM WHOLE EARTH CATALOG

1985 1990 1995 1996 2000 2005 2006 2010 2015 2020 2025 2030 2035 2040 2045 2050 **2055** 2060 2065 2070 2075 2080 2085 2090 2095 2100 2200

BOTTOM LINE: VIRTUAL SEX SLAVES ALREADY EXIST, BUT THEY ARE EITHER PAY-BY-THE-MINUTE PHONE PERSONALITIES OR COMPUTER GAME ANIMATIONS. IT WILL BE 2055 BEFORE ONE CAN ACTUALLY BOOT UP, SUIT UP, AND DO IT WITH A SOFTWARE SEX PROGRAM.

As Philip K. Dick's novel, *Do Androids Dream of Electric Sheep?* opens, detective Rick Deckard and his wife, Iran, are having a quarrel over the settings on their Penfield mood organs. He had set his to bring him from slumber to fully awake and chipper, while she remains groggy, no better off than if she'd been stirred by a conventional alarm clock.

"'You set your Penfield too weak,' he said to her. 'I'll reset it and you'll be awake and – '

"'Keep your hand off my settings.' Her voice held bitter sharpness. 'I don't want to be awake.'"

This passage reveals Dick's particular genius to not only anticipate the kinds of technologies we might embrace, but discern their limits as well. Still, even if we reject mood management devices in the future, few of us deny the *appeal* of selecting a mood at will, and then either swallowing a pill, drinking a tonic, or hooking up for an electric jolt to effectively dial-a-mood. The success of Prozac hints at the potential consumer demand, as does some people's near-addiction to television, audio/visual tapes, radio, and other light/sound devices as stimulants and/or pacifiers.

To truly dial-a-mood, however, Dr. John Morgan says we will have to find a means of effecting stimulation within the brain's limbic system, where sensory integration occurs and moods are believed to originate. This would require that a microscopic system be either delivered to or surgically implanted in the nucleus accumbens, technology that remains in R & D today. Shulgin speculates, however, that such a device will be quickly prohibited.

Fluoxetine: Industry chart on the drug that named a nation, Prozac. *www.cs.umn.edu/Research/GIMME/ISAP/incoming/drugs/Fluoxetine.html* More complete discussion of Prozac and serotonin. Prozac's effect involves the blocking of serotonin at the level of neural synapse in the brain. *www.arach-net.com/~jlyon/biochem/results.html* Mood Disorders: A learned essay on mood disorders by Doug Vartanoff. *www.umd.umich.edu/~marcyb/to6/psych/vartanoff.html* The Negative Ion Homepage: The calm after a storm, the crush of a waterfall, a pine forest; they all give off negative ions – airborne Prozac according to this discussion of drug-free highs and lows. *supermall.com/negion/negion.html*

1985

1990

1995

1996 TIMOTHY LEARY, PH.D., PHILOSOPHER

2000 ANDREW WEIL, M.D., AUTHOR OF *SPONTANEOUS HEALING AND NATURAL HEALTH, NATURAL MEDICINE*

2000 ALEXANDER SHULGIN, M.D., CHEMIST/PHARMACOLOGIST, UNIVERSITY OF CALIFORNIA, BERKELEY, AND CO-AUTHOR OF *PIHKAL: A CHEMICAL LOVE STORY*

2005

2010

2015

2020

2025

2030

2035

2040

2045

2050 MICHAEL ALDRICH, PH.D., CURATOR, FITZ HUGH LUDLOW MEMORIAL LIBRARY

2055

2060

2065

2070

2075

2080

2085

2090

2095

2225

3094 JOHN MORGAN, M.D., PROFESSOR OF PHARMACOLOGY, CITY UNIVERSITY OF NEW YORK, AND MEMBER OF THE ADVISORY BOARD OF THE DRUG POLICY FOUNDATION

BOTTOM LINE: WE ALREADY SELECT OUR MOODS TO SOME EXTENT, BUT TECHNOLOGY THAT WILL ENABLE US TO DIAL-A-MOOD WITH CERTAINTY WILL

Communist Party USA: homepage of the Communist Party, including electronic versions of *The People Weekly World: www.hartford-hwp.com/cp-usa/index.html* Third-Party and Independent Candidates in American Politics: Wallace, Anderson, and Perot: A forum for four professors who discuss also-rans for the presidency not affiliated with either the elephants or the donkeys. *epn.org/psq/psqbra.html* The Crisis of the Two-Party System: An essay by Jarvis Tyner on why the two-party system fails U.S. Voters. *www.hartford-hwp.com/cp-usa/paz.html* Third-Party Campaign Launch Extremely Difficult: An analysis written by Mark Keenan based largely on input from James Thurber, director of American University's Center for Congressional and Presidential Studies. *www.usia.gov/elections/3rdpties.htm*

Millions connected by PC and modem to their legislators and to the ballot box; Capitol Hill debates transformed into virtual town meetings; the U.S. government "reengineered"; "the-lesser-of-two-evils" presidential elections finally abolished by computer networks that favor diversity and lower the economic barriers of entry into national politics – these are but some of the visions of democracy in a digital age. Still, ask most political observers today and they'll tell you you're dreaming if you expect any of these things to happen soon.

For one thing, the numbers of people online are too scant to rival the influence of television networks. Until the Internet is connected to and used by people in 90 percent of homes, says Gerald Posner, the networks will still exert the greatest influence on elections. Thus, before online exchanges can alter the status quo, Posner and others insist, millions more will not only have to get connected to the Net, but also actually participate in politics online.

Other observers, including Jean Bethke Elshtain, are dubious about the promise communications technology holds for our political system, even with time. "Right now the two parties are basically fund-raising entities that throw galas every four years," Elshtain says. "But you have to keep in mind that they are internally diverse; they are coalitions, and coalitions are hard work." Forging new alliances with modems, she says, may happen around single issues, but will not necessarily undermine the Democrats or Republicans on Election Day.

And yet, if communications technology won't easily recast the elephant and donkey show, are there other factors that may unravel the two-party system's lock on the White House? Only one of the pundits we interviewed doubted that an independent or third-party candidate will capture the White House in the next 30 years. "With the two parties we are seeing a trend of mediocrity coming to the top," reflects Posner, "and whenever you have weak candidates from the two parties, it opens it up to independents."

Like Posner, several of our experts note that a viable third-party or independent candidate must either have the money to buy television time (as Ross Perot does), or have in their favor the celebrity factor (a film career, for example) so that television cameras will cover them as soon as they announce their candidacy. Still, one independent election victory might not spell a permanent end to the two-party system.

"There are few voters who won't abandon one party or the other over one issue or another," observes Jon Katz. "Membership doesn't really demand anything or mean anything…. The moral part is really what they're about." Katz notes that the government relies on the two-party system, and that few government officials share the technolibertarians' desire to see them eliminated. Posits Katz, "The government totally depends on there being something like [a two-party system], and there is no coherent replacement in sight, so I'd say [the two parties] will limp along in a hollow shell for years."

EDWIN DIAMOND, "MEDIUM COOL" COLUMNIST, *POLITICS NOW*, AND CO-AUTHOR, *FROM WHITE HOUSE TO YOUR HOUSE*

GERALD POSNER, ATTORNEY, AND AUTHOR OF *CITIZEN PEROT: HIS LIFE & TIMES*

JON KATZ, NOVELIST AND MEDIA CRITIC FOR *WIRED* AND *HOTWIRED*, AND AUTHOR OF *VIRTUOUS REALITY*

JEAN BETHKE ELSHTAIN, PROFESSOR OF SOCIAL AND POLITICAL ETHICS, UNIVERSITY OF CHICAGO, AND AUTHOR OF *DEMOCRACY ON TRIAL*

2000 2005 2010 2015 2020 2025 2030 2035 2040 2045 2050 2055 2060 2065 2070 2075 2080 2085 2090 2095 2100 2105 2110

UNLIKELY   UNLIKELY   UNLIKELY   UNLIKELY

JETPACKS FOR PERSONAL TRANSPORTATION

UNLIKELY

URLS/FURTHER READING

NASA-CIT Jet propulsion Laboratory: Homepage of the NASA propulsion lab with news flashes, a run down of missions and instruments and a handy, "frequently asked questions" link. *www.jpl.nasa.gov/* Bell Rocket Belt: An entertaining history of the jetpack with schematic drawings and photos from test flights in the 1960s. *www.prysm.com/~jnuts/rocktbelt.htm* Transportation Research Board: Homepage of the Transportation Research Board, a clearing house/brain trust for innovations in personal transport. For the sober researcher. *www.nas.edu/trb/*

If you're content with a 28-second joy ride, then look no further than the American Flying Belt produced in Houston, Texas. In a 1995 demonstration, William (Bill) Suitor, the "original rocketeer" who charmed audiences in the 1960s, strapped on a new model of the Bell rocket pack invented by Doug Malewicki and blasted off. The fuel, as before, was hydrogen peroxide. The current model, sold as a kit, is available by mail order.

Fun as it is to see the jetpack attempt a comeback, the experts we consulted predict that neither the rocket packs developed by Malewicki nor the ones tested by the U.S. military will ever make the transition from novelty to preferred mode of personal transport. According to Richard Klimisch, they are more likely to be found in high-tech toy chests than in carports. Thomas B. Deen explains that their costs are simply too high for personal use, and Noah Rifkin cites "unknown market demand" as a barrier to investment and R & D.

If there is any hope that jetpacks will be the motorcycle of the 21st century, it lies in a new source of power. Steven E. Shladover predicts that jetpacks will not become popular unless nuclear fusion makes energy cheap enough to make jetpacks economical.

1985
1990
1995
2000 RICHARD L. KLIMISCH, PH.D., VICE PRESIDENT OF ENGINEERING, AMERICAN AUTOMOBILE MANUFACTURERS ASSOCIATION
2005
2010
2015
2020 RUPERT WELCH, EDITOR, *INSIDE DOT AND TRANSPORTATION WEEK*
2025
2030
2035
2040
2045
2050 THOMAS B. DEEN, EXECUTIVE DIRECTOR, TRANSPORTATION RESEARCH BOARD
2055
2060
2065
2070
2075
2080
2085
2090
2095
2100
2105

UNLIKELY NOAH RIFKIN, DIRECTOR OF TECHNOLOGY DEPLOYMENT, UNITED STATES DEPARTMENT OF TRANSPORTATION

NEVER STEVEN E. SHLADOVER, ACTING DIRECTOR, CALIFORNIA PARTNERS FOR ADVANCED TRANSIT AND HIGHWAYS

ORBITING SOLAR POWER PLANT

UNLIKELY

Will we look back decades from now and shake our heads in disbelief – and perhaps with relief – that we voluntarily stopped relying on fossil fuels for 80 percent of our total energy needs? Or will future generations condemn us because 90 percent of the CO_2 emissions thought responsible for the greenhouse effect came from burning fossil fuels – at a time when we were already well-equipped to harvest the energy in the sun's rays.

Although our experts on solar power are among the first to emphasize the need for alternative energy sources to replace fossil fuels (see also "Hemp-Based Auto Fuel," page 71, and "Solar Power to the People," page 41), they're not so sure an orbiting solar power station will be the solution to humans' increasing energy needs here on Earth.

The proposed scenario is this: A satellite with supersensitive solar panels gets blasted into Earth orbit, where in the absence of the atmosphere solar energy is eight times more intense than it is on the Earth's surface. The energy would be collected and stored in on-board batteries and then beamed via microwaves to rectennæ on the Earth's surface. (Joseph Hawkins, an engineer-professor at the University of Alaska, Fairbanks, has designed a system for the microwave transfer of solar energy, called PowerSat.) Once received by terrestrial power stations, the energy would be converted to AC and fed into existing power grids.

While Frank Goodman believes a small-scale demonstration of a space-based solar power generator transmitting energy to Earth could happen within 30 years, most of our experts agree with Christopher Flavin, who contends that at a cost of US$100,000 per kilogram of payload to put something into orbit, it will always be cheaper to generate solar power on Earth. Our sources at the National Renewable Energy Laboratory add that even if a space-based solar power plant is technologically feasible, it's environmentally risky (beaming microwave energy to earth that could stray) and would create a single point of failure (the Earth-based station). "It would be much like routing every Internet node through a single, central office," they say. And while a space-based power generator may be an idea whose time has already passed, Donald Osborn points out that it is "an important concept because it helped us broaden our thinking about the potentials of solar power."

SPS2000: In both Japanese and English, a proposal for a solar power satellite. sps.tksc.dc.jp/index.html PowerSat: At the University of Alaska, a proposal for a device that would allow the microwave transfer of energy gathered from the sun. asgp.uafjsoe.alaska.edu/researched.dir/adp.dir/powersat.html Solar Power Satellites: Seth Potter writes that solar based power is "an idea whose time has come." www.skypoint.com/members/rab/sps.html Space Solar Power: A Feasible Resource?: A thoughtful piece by John Mankins weighing the pros and cons, circa 1995. nctn.oact.hq.nasa.gov/STI/Innovation3s/Space_Power.html 2 kW Solar Dynamic Space Power System: An impressive prototype. powerweb.lerc.nasa.gov/soldyn/DOC/SDGTD.html

FRANK GOODMAN, MANAGER, PHOTOVOLTAIC TECHNOLOGY AND APPLICATIONS, ELECTRIC POWER RESEARCH INSTITUTE

MARK FITZGERALD, COMMUNICATIONS COORDINATOR, NATIONAL RENEWABLE ENERGY LABORATORY (NREL)

CHRISTOPHER FLAVIN, VICE PRESIDENT FOR RESEARCH, WORLDWATCH INSTITUTE, AND CO-AUTHOR OF POWER SURGE

DONALD OSBORN, SUPERVISOR, SACRAMENTO MUNICIPAL UTILITY DISTRICT'S SOLAR PROGRAM

STEVEN STRONG, PRESIDENT, SOLAR DESIGN ASSOCIATES, INC.

THOMAS SUREK, PHOTOVOLTAICS DIVISION, NREL

2000
2005
2010
2015
2020
2025
2030
2035
2040
2045
2050
2055
2060
2065
2070
2075
2080
2085
2090
2095
2100
2105

UNLIKELY
UNLIKELY
UNLIKELY
UNLIKELY
UNLIKELY

AN INTERACTIVE TV IN EVERY HOME

NEVER

URLS/FURTHER READING
Interactive TV: The boxscores. bcn.boulder.co.us/pdxflood/teleport-smac/cable4.html I & TCom: Homepage for a software company that developed Domotev, a user-interface for the television. www.hospitalitynet.nl/itcom/interact.htm The Intercast Industry Group: They've seen the future of ITV and it's on a PC. www.intercast.org/

How many times have you heard about interactive television (ITV) or any of its proposed "killer applications" – movies-on-demand, say, or online shopping? (See pages 5 and 69, respectively.) Enough times that your idea of being interactive is putting your foot through your television set? If so, you're forgiven.

According to all but one of the experts we consulted about computer interfaces, the idea of ITV should be read its last rites. For one thing, it's next to impossible to say just what an interactive television would be: A set that plays digital video? A set that also functions as a computer monitor? A high-tech set-top box that allows the TV to alternate between several functions?

Even though set-top boxes continue to improve, have been adopted by hotels and nursing homes, and the hype surrounding interactivity continues to spawn new catchphrases like "Web TV" – a TV that would allow viewers to browse the World Wide Web – the experts we polled don't see the long-term viability of either using devices to make TVs "smart" when PCs will always be smarter, or trying to make PCs function more like TVs when millions of people already own both.

More specifically, software tools like Java and OLE and search engines like Yahoo! and HotBots will make Web access more intelligent, not less so, and from this observation our panelists make the point that people turn to their TVs and computers for different purposes – and with good reason. The first allows you to *veg out;* the second requires active participation; the former allows you to join a program already in progess; the latter doesn't do anything until you give it a command.

Nevertheless, major companies, including IBM, Apple, and most notably Zenith, are investing in televisions that come equipped with modems and Ethernet connections in the belief they will be popular enough to penetrate the market by 50 percent in five to seven years. If so, John Markoff will have to eat his hat. "TV," he wrote with finality, "is dead."

1985 1990 1995 2000 2003 2005 2010 2015 2020 2025 2030 2035 2040 2045 2050 2055 2060 2065 2070 2075 2080 2085 2090 2095

2003 DON NORMAN, VICE PRESIDENT, ADVANCED TECHNOLOGY, APPLE COMPUTER

UNLIKELY DENISE CARUSO, DIGITAL COMMERCE COLUMNIST FOR *THE NEW YORK TIMES*, EXECUTIVE PRODUCER OF THE SPOTLIGHT CONFERENCE ON INTERACTIVE MEDIA

NEVER ROBERT JACOBSON, FOUNDER AND PRESIDENT, WORLDESIGN, INC.

NEVER JOHN MARKOFF, REPORTER, *THE NEW YORK TIMES*, AUTHOR OF *CYBERPUNK: OUTLAWS AND HACKERS ON THE COMPUTER FRONTIER*

THE PAPERLESS OFFICE
NEVER

URLS/FURTHER READING
The Paperless Design Studio, GSAP: Going digital changes the way architects draft their projects, and where. *www.arch.columbia.edu:80/DDL/paperless/NEWSLINE.html* NewtonSource: A personal data assistant (PDA) aiming to replace the writing tablet. *www.newtonsource.com/index.html* OmniGo: A rival PDA to the Newton. *www.axxis.com/~mfine/fbabout.html* Pen Vision Information Systems, Inc.: A line of portable computing devices. *www.penvision.com/*

ROBERT JACOBSON, FOUNDER AND PRESIDENT, WORLDESIGN, INC. (50% PAPERLESS)

JOHN MARKOFF, REPORTER, *THE NEW YORK TIMES*, AUTHOR OF *CYBERPUNKS: OUTLAWS AND HACKERS ON THE COMPUTER FRONTIER*

DON NORMAN, VICE PRESIDENT, ADVANCED TECHNOLOGY, APPLE COMPUTER

DENISE CARUSO, DIGITAL COMMERCE COLUMNIST FOR *THE NEW YORK TIMES*, EXECUTIVE PRODUCER OF THE SPOTLIGHT CONFERENCE ON INTERACTIVE MEDIA

Only ten years ago, when laptops were cumbersome enough to be mistaken for luggage, futurists were already heralding the day when we would all go paperless: instead of faxes, email; instead of notes in the margin of yellow legal pads, Newtons or other digital personal assistants; instead of a Filofax, Franklin Quest planner, or Day-at-a-Glance, a programmable wristwatch complete with engagement calendar.

Well, all the technologies that were to replace paper have arrived – and paper remains. Bill Ziff, from computer trade-publishing giant Ziff-Davis, put it succinctly when he noted that if we had been living in a CRT (cathode ray tube) culture for the last two hundred years and someone had just invented paper, they would still be considered a hero. As those who've tried to go paperless know, it is next to impossible to be a paperless island in a sea of paper, and even though some people may approach a paperless existence, our panelists say it'll be 2005 before most of us can realize a 50 percent reduction in paper use. In his most optimistic projection, Don Norman predicts we'll be only 80 percent "papyrus-free" by 2009.

Nevertheless, John Markoff maintains that the paperless office is inevitable. Says Markoff: "Flat panel displays are on the same cost performance curve as other semiconductors. Resolution will surpass paper in the next five years."

| 1990 | 1995 | 2000 | 2005 | 2005 | 2010 | 2015 | 2020 | 2025 | 2030 | 2035 | 2040 | 2045 | 2050 | 2055 | 2060 | 2065 | 2070 | 2075 | 2080 | 2085 | 2090 | 2095 | 2100 | 2105 | 2110 | NEVER |

BOTTOM LINE: PAPER IS TOO HIGHLY ENTRENCHED IN OUR CULTURE TO FACE

HUMAN CLONES
NEVER

Human Genome Project information: A well-organized assortment of links introducing the Human Genome Project and other genome research. www.ornl.gov /TechResources/Human_Genome/home.html National Center for Human Genome Research: Site with excellent background on HGP and related research, beautifully illustrated. www.nchgr.nih.gov/ Site maintained by the U.S. Department of Energy. www.er.doe.gov/production/oher/hug_top.html Stanford Human Genome Center: Homepage highlighting this institution's efforts. shgc_www.stanford.edu/ The Human Genome Project: Where Will It Take Us?: An analysis of the HGP with a discussion of what it's good for. www.healthtouch.com/level1/leaflets/48601/hhrr010.htm

FRANK LEE, PH.D., MOLECULAR BIOLOGIST

CYNTHIA ROBBINS-ROTH, PH.D., EDITOR-IN-CHIEF OF BIOVENTURE PUBLISHING, INC.

DR. DAVID E. R. SUTHERLAND, M. D., PH.D., PROFESSOR OF SURGERY AND DIRECTOR OF THE PANCREAS TRANSPLANT PROGRAM, UNIVERSITY OF MINNESOTA

Imagine running into the twin you never knew you had – or discovering that there are dozens of your "twins" out there. Or imagine a world where batches of 96 "twins" are bred to do society's dirty work. (Okay, the last one's already been written.)

To date, cloning humans has remained beyond our control; unless, of course, you count the imaginations of writers like Aldous Huxley or Rod Serling. Still, many of the biomedical researchers we consulted consider human cloning technically feasible, if potentially terrifying.

A major boon to human cloning will be the completion of the Human Genome Project, itself the subject of a great deal of hype. The stated goal of the Human Genome Project is to develop a "map" of human DNA, to identify the location, structure, and function of the estimated thousands of human genes. In the United States, this project gets support from both the U.S. Department of Energy and the National Institutes of Health. The project's annual operating budget of more than US$200 million is justified by the prospect of understanding and treating "more than 4,000 genetic diseases that afflict mankind." Asked when they thought the Human Genome Project would be complete, Cynthia Robbins-Roth said 2001; Frank Lee, 2005; and Dr. David E. R. Sutherland, 2000. Says Robbins-Roth, "We need to discover cheaper and faster methods to sequence the three billion base pairs of the human genome." She looks forward to "the real point of this": figuring out the biological function of the encoded proteins.

Of course, a complete map of human DNA is not needed to commence cloning, and where cloning is concerned, our experts insist that technical feasibility should not be the chief concern. Opines Sutherland, "Here is where we need the Luddites."

1990 1995 2000 2004 2005 2010 2015 2020 2025 2030 2035 2040 2045 2050 2055 2060 2065 2070 2075 2080 2085 2090 2095 2100 2105 **NEVER** NEVER

BOTTOM LINE: ALTHOUGH MANY RESEARCHERS THINK HUMAN CLONING WILL BECOME TECHNICALLY FEASIBLE, IT WON'T BE SANCTIONED IF CURRENT ETHICAL OPPOSITION ENDURES.

VIRTUAL WAR

NEVER

Virtual War and Virtual Peace: "The Postmodern Alternative for Conflict Resolution." *www.princeton.edu/~rlasalle/virtual.html* Defense Advanced Research Projects Agency: Homepage of the central R & D arm of the U.S. Department of Defense. *www.arpa.mil/* Division 44: Where to learn about the U.S. government's Simulation and Human-Systems Technology Division. *froggie.nosc.mil/* Federation of American Scientists: Homepage of FAS, scientists who want to make sure science serves, rather than harms, humans. *www.fas.org/* Computer Generated Forces: An institute where they develop simulation programs for training. *www.ist.ucf.edu/~IST /labs/cgf/* Los Alamos National Laboratory. *www.lanl.gov/Public/Welcome.html*

JOHN ALEXANDER, PH.D., RETIRED U.S. ARMY COLONEL, AND HEAD OF THE NONLETHAL WEAPONRY PROGRAM AT LOS ALAMOS NATIONAL LABORATORY

RICHARD GARWIN, CHAIR OF THE FAS FUND, THE RESEARCH ARM OF THE FEDERATION OF AMERICAN SCIENTISTS

"What if they gave a war and nobody came?" What if computer games didn't only simulate troop engagements, aerial dog fights, and intercontinental ballistic missile strikes, but actually *replaced* them? What if, instead of producing casualties and scorched earth, we waged wars on-screen, deciding previously mortal conflicts without bloodshed?

A nice idea, say the experts we consulted, but their conclusion is that *it ain't gonna happen*. In fact, in discussion after discussion, both on the record and off, the response to the prospects of a "virtual war" was simply this: virtual wars have already been waged and continue to be waged in the media, where the term describes the machines of propaganda.

By way of example, our experts noted that one of the clichés of the media coverage of the U.S.-led Gulf War in 1991 was the resemblance of the action to a "Nintendo War."

The comments of our experts reflect several points of view. From Richard Garwin came the assertion that the Cuban Missile Crisis of 1962 was a form of virtual war, a situation in which "stand-off or face-down [was] achieved by a shared view of outcomes." From Manuel De Landa came a more literal interpretation. If what we mean by virtual war is conflict that would be settled as if by computer chess, DeLanda says, then it will never come to pass. John Alexander asserts that virtual war, whether defined as simulation, propaganda, or high-tech detente, is a reality today. Finally, a producer and engineer of multimedia simulations suggests that another aspect of virtual war might well be Information Age sabotage, in which the goal of the saboteur is to destroy information vital to his or her enemy.

MANUEL DE LANDA, AUTHOR OF *WAR IN THE AGE OF INTELLIGENT MACHINES*

1985 1990 1995 1996 1996 2000 2005 2010 2015 2020 2025 2030 2035 2040 2045 2050 2055 2060 2065 2070 2075 2080 2085 2090 2095 2100

NEVER

CREDITS

CREDITS

INDEX

INDEX

INDEX